Anyone who has ever don_ with *giants*: giant issues, giant problems, and giant challenges. Pastor Jamie Jones has written an amazing book that will awaken the giant-killer in you! Read it and get ready for victory. Never forget this: Nobody remembers who the giant killed, but everyone remembers who killed the giant!
— **Jim Raley**
Lead Pastor of Calvary Christian Center, Ormond Beach, Florida, and Author of *Hell's Spells* and *Dream Killers*

Are you ready to kill the giant that has stood in the way of all God has called you to accomplish? Then read this book by my friend, Jamie Jones. *Kill the Giant* will awaken your purpose and destiny to realize that the things you have considered to be hard to kill can be defeated if you will become bold, tenacious, and hungry for more. God deliberately chooses "nobodies"—men and women that culture overlooks, exploits, and abuses—to expose the hollow pretensions of the "somebodies." You are God's representative who could be used to shift a nation and restore hope to the oppressed!
— **Pat Schatzline**
Evangelist, Remnant Ministries International, Author of many books including Best-seller *Restore the Roar*

Pastor Jamie Jones is a passionate, on fire, anointed man of God. This new book is an explosive collection of time-tested biblical wisdom, broken down into easy-to-apply action steps. It's strategically designed to encourage, inspire, and help anyone who is facing inner giants, going through trials and tribulations, or who just desire to walk in the fullness of God's blessing.
-Dr. Billy Alsbrooks
Author, *Blessed and Unstoppable*

Dr. Jamie Jones not only writes about defeating giants, he lives this message. His ministry and message is one of helping people become "more than conquerors" and live as an "overcomer." I encourage you to get this book, read it, and live it. God has *more* for you!
— **Dr. Scott Young**
Lead Pastor, Church of Hope, Sarasota, Florida

This is the one book you need to read right now! All of us are just one piece of information away from massive breakthrough; and this book is full of golden nuggets that will propel you into the destiny for which you've always dreamed. *Kill the Giant* gives a proven strategy to overcome the giants in your life and experience overflowing abundance!
— **Jamey Paugh**
CEO, Paugh International

When Joyce and I began our missionary career in 1966, I would have been overjoyed to have received Jamie Jones's *Kill the Giant*. We were facing giants in the land of Spain where there was no religious freedom to share Christ, plant churches, or open a Bible school. Jamie has written the book that every Christian, pastor, and missionary needs to read and *reread*! His insights are giant-killing strategies that, once applied, brings total victory. This book needs not only to be purchased, but to be given out by the dozens. Jamie has written what he practices, and this is the key!
— **Sam Johnson**
Executive Director, Priority One

Dr. Jamie Jones masterfully reveals the answer to the timeless question: how does one kill their giants? From defeating doubt to dreaming again, this book will eradicate your fears and escalate your faith. *Kill the Giant* is an unassailable weapon in the hand of every person who's destined to defeat what will no longer defeat them.

— **Pastor Juan Wilder**
Impact One Church, Capitol Heights, Maryland

The Devil will ensure that in your life you will always have a battle; and through this book, you will learn how to overcome every time. Pastor Jamie has detailed that the giants in your life are not meant to simply be dealt with, but to be defeated. Make *Kill the Giant* a priority, because your giant, just like Goliath and the Israelites, is calling you out, saying, "Who will fight me?" This book will give you the strength and courage to fight and win!

— **James Jones III**
Minister of Youth, Trinity Church, Deltona, Florida

Kill the Giant is an easy-to-read book that will challenge you. So many of us have big dreams but never actually accomplish them. This book will give you the tools you need to reach for what seems impossible.

— **Kristen Alvarez**
CEO, Love Dearly Ministry

Another wonderful book by Pastor Jamie Jones! I so enjoy how he writes in everyday language and how he integrates scripture into the many experiences we *all* share. Jamie helps readers to change and grow in their faith using personal and biblical stories. *Kill The Giant* will surely be a blessing to many.

— **Jermaine J. Rodriguez**
Lead Pastor MyChurch, Jacksonville, Florida

There are plenty of teachers who can tell us the way, but our world is sorely lacking fathers who can *show* us the way. As a true spiritual father, Jamie Jones has pioneered a path that we can follow to kill the giants in our lives. This is a battle-tested blueprint for success!

— **Brent Simpson**
Lead Pastor, ARISE Church, Brandon, Florida

At some point in our lives, many of us have faced the overwhelming fear of failure and insecurity. We hide behind the unknown, telling ourselves that we can't achieve our dreams, when, in fact, we haven't even made an effort to try. I am so thankful for Pastor Jamie's latest book, *Kill the Giant*, which not only motivates the reader to be an overcomer but equips them along the way. This book is a metaphorical stone pulled from the river of hope to be used in a sling of effort slung towards the giants attacking your purpose.

— **Timothy McCain**
Opening Eyes Ministries, Author of *Crowns Are Greater than Trophies* and *This Is Your Chance*

There is one thing that we all have in common, and that is that at some point in our lives, we will face a giant. Pastor Jamie Jones's *Kill the Giant* not only offers the inspiration to get started, but gives practical steps needed to overcome the cycle of defeat. Having known him for over twenty years, I know that this is a book he and his family have lived. I highly recommend it to anyone who wants to move forward—starting right now!

— **Bryan Rosenbarger**
Lead Pastor, Grace Chapel, Loxahatchee, Florida

In my twenty-two year Air Force career, I knew many warriors. The best of them knew how to take a seemingly impossible mission, break it down to its many steps and tasks, come up with a strategy of attack, and then pick the right people, the right plan, and the right weapons to enable our victory. In his new book, *Kill the Giant*, Pastor Jamie uses a similar strategy with a step-by-step, common-sense approach that will enable your victory—whatever your struggle! Read it, absorb it, then pick up your newly-acquired weapons, charge into combat, and win!

— **Dr. Dennis Robinson**
Lt. Col, USAF, retired

Pastor Jamie Jones has once again hit a "home run" in his new book *Kill the Giant*. His insight into God's Word along with his personal experiences challenge us to not only recognize the root problem of our struggles but face them head-on, ultimately fulfilling our God-given call. *Kill the Giant* will motivate, inspire, and stir up your passion to conquer complacency and intimidation. If you desire to walk with new courage and commitment to live a life worthy of the calling you have received, *Kill the Giant* is a must read!

— **Susan Pippin**
Author of *Susan's Coffee Break* and *Which Ring Will You Fight In?*

Pastor Jamie Jones uses his latest book, *Kill the Giant*, to bring you to a moment of truth of how badly you want a God-filled life. Are you positioned and prepared to confront and conquer your giant? Are you ready to effectively overcome your obstacles and fully trust God? Read the book. Live out the book. I promise that you will never be the same.

— **Mark Nelson, Regional Director**
Samaritan's Purse

Pastor Jamie Jones has once again opened a topic at the heart of the struggle many face in their walk with Christ. The giants that have obtained access into our life continue to rob us of the plan and purpose God has for us. I believe close attention to the truths and guidelines offered in this book will allow you to clearly face and eliminate the giants that infest your life.
— **Ken Pippin**
Finish Strong Ministries, Author of *Boats and Bait*

kill the
giant.

Defeat the Thing
That's Defeating You

Jamie Jones

Dedication

This book is dedicated to all the hardworking people out there who, in spite of life's problems, absolutely refuse to quit. This would include single parents, those who have experienced devastating loss, those who have either defeated or are currently fighting life-threatening illness, those fighting mental or physical challenges, people born into disadvantaged situations, and more. You are the true definition of the word *hero*. This writing is dedicated to you. You are the true Giant Killers!

Contents

Acknowledgments

To my wife, Michelle, you are the epitome of a giant-killer and serve as a major inspiration for this writing.

To my three kids, Kristen, James, and Joshua: I am so proud of you. You are all world-changers, and the enemy will not soon forget your influence on the earth.

I would like to thank all who contributed by praying and supporting me in making this book possible.

To my little Ember Jane, you are a giant-killer in the making. Thank you for making my life more complete.

To my parents and grandparents, whose impact on my life has allowed me to expect for more and believe for bigger.

To my staff, thank you for your hard work and support during this project.

Trinity Church, thank you for your love, support, and faithfulness.

Jesus, thank You for saving me and allowing me the honor of preaching Your Word.

Foreword

When you read a book, it is always for the same person. You. The reader. Books are not for the author; they are for the reader. When I write a book, I write it from my perspective, from my experience, from what I have learned, but it is always written for others. It is always the same: it is for the reader to gain knowledge, wisdom, principles, strategies, power, or encouragement.

Although books are written with the same basic intention, they do not always serve the same *purpose*. Some books will help you in your relationships, while some are pure entertainment. Some books push you to go further in life, and some teach you principles of success. Some books will provide you with strategies for your business. No matter what the purpose of the book, the intention behind writing it must be to make a difference in the reader's life.

This is what Jamie Jones has done in *Kill the Giant*. He has written a book that will positively impact your life and make a difference. I've known Jamie for many years, and he is an encourager—he is always encouraging others to reach for their goals and keep dreaming. He urges them to dig deeper within

Scripture to apply the principles found there to their everyday life.

Have you ever felt like giving up? Have you ever wondered if the dreams you once had would ever come to pass? Have you ever thought: *Why keep dreaming?* Have you ever doubted yourself? Have you ever wondered if God could still use you? Have you ever wondered if you were enough? Then this book is for you!

Jamie takes a realistic approach to addressing all of these questions. He gives you strategies for how to overcome fear and doubt, how to dream bigger, and encourages you to never give up. He shares personal stories and pertinent wisdom about struggles he has endured and how he overcame them. He talks openly about belief systems that he had to change. He is raw, he is real, and he is vulnerable.

As you go through the first chapter, you will begin to identify and breakdown debilitating barriers. If you're struggling with doubt and discouragement, he will speak to you in the next few chapters about how you can believe in yourself once again! He shows you how to be tenacious and go after your dreams and not accept *no* from anyone. Finally, he shows you how prepare for the lethal fight and emerge victorious!

I would advise you to read this book with intentionality. Take notes, dive into the stories he shares, and apply them to your life. If you will do this, I know you will start to believe in yourself again. Each one of us was created for greatness. I highly recommend this book to anyone who is ready to kill their giants and grab the life of greatness they were born to live.

— Dr. Dave Martin
Your Success Coach, Author of *The 12 Traits of the Greats*

Introduction

So much writing has been done on the subject of giants, both mythical and real. Do we really need another book on how to slay a giant? My thinking behind this book was not to try and add to what others have already written, as that would be pretty arrogant, but rather to create a resource to equip people for success.

The world is full of giant-killers: those who are willing to face almost insurmountable odds and still find a way to win. The techniques they employ are transferable to most anyone willing to dig down deep within themselves and go to battle. These people aren't super-humans; they just believe both in themselves and the Almighty.

We cannot avoid seasons of doubt and discouragement or moments when we hear devastating news that knocks the wind out of our sails. But in those seasons and moments, the decisions we make and actions that follow can either defeat the giant or allow him to continue to taunt and plague our lives.

I have read about and witnessed firsthand those who have been able to defeat their giant. It is never easy. It takes great focus and an enormous amount of persistence.

Nevertheless, even with all of the challenges, the giant *can* be defeated.

Each of the following chapters contain some practical helps: things you can do right now to begin to change your situation. As you read, I strongly encourage you to take the time to utilize these keys to assist you in reaching your breakthrough. You may have been on the receiving end of intimidation for quite a while, but it stops here and it stops now. Turn these pages if you dare. It's time to kill the giant!

Chapter 1:
Hard to Kill

Weeds! I wonder how many millions of dollars have been made by those in the business of killing them. When you walk down the lawn care aisle of your local home-improvement store, there's more variations in weed killer than there are cars on a used-car lot. There are sprays, powders, granules, and who knows what else. There are even pre-emergent and post-emergent weed killers. There's so much to choose from that you almost need some sort of degree in horticulture just to make the purchase. As you make your selection though, know this: Regardless of how much money you spend on killing weeds, there is one thing you can bet on: No matter what—they will come back.

I have some cracks in the driveway of my home. These small cracks provide just enough space for pesky little weeds to pop through on a recurring basis. I have pulled them up very gently and meticulously, so as not to break them and leave any of the root behind. I usually get a few brief days of satisfaction, and then with the same rhythmic certainty of sunrise and sunset, there they are again. I eventually gave up trying to pull them up. I am convinced that pulling them is an exercise in futility! Now when I mow my yard I just take the weed trimmer and cut them off as close as possible to give myself a small window of weed-free enjoyment.

Sometimes the difficulties we endure in life seem a lot like this recurring weed scenario. We pray, we seek advice, we cry, we fight, and we stay at it, but there are some things we deal with that are very stubborn and hard to overcome. The majority of the issues we deal with daily are things we can handle and navigate, but there are some things that seem to exhaust all our energy and drain us emotionally. These complex issues are not simple tasks or easy decisions; these problems gain momentum and build mountains. In fact, they can become so deeply ingrained in our psyche that they appear too difficult to overcome.

I remember hearing stories of the mythical giants of ancient Greek literature and folklore. My imagination would run absolutely wild as I tried to picture what these beasts might actually look like: the famed cyclops who had only one large eye, or the wildly disturbing story of Jack and the Beanstalk, complete with a flesh-eating giant with a keen sense of smell. Of course, Greek mythological giants are only the product of pen and paper and a zealous writer itching to write a new fable, whereas some giants we face in life are all too real.

Life is full of many giants that we are forced to face. Most of the time, they are only defeated after perseverance and sometimes extensive collateral damage.

Chapter 1: Hard to Kill

These giants take many different forms and can be a bit unpredictable, but one thing you can always count on is that a giant never dies easily. These giants threaten people's emotional stability, self-confidence, and can even affect their physical stamina. When people go through hard stress and face seemingly insurmountable obstacles, it is not without a personal toll.

Any couple who has been through a divorce will tell you that the pain, anxiety, and uncertainties of the future could certainly be likened to a giant. The decisions that need to be made and the future that is up in the air can leave people with a sense of helplessness and pain that is hard to even describe. The legal red tape and financial stress is more than most ever bargained for.

Life is full of giants, but often the most difficult giant we will ever face will be the giant of self-doubt.

The drug addict who has overcome his or her addiction can give testimony to the fact that conquering their addiction was much harder than they had ever anticipated. The sleepless nights, the physical and financial repercussions, and the pain of withdrawal are the stuff of nightmares. Rehab centers are full of people who have tried over and over, but are hoping that this time they will have a different outcome.

Life is full of giants, but often the most difficult giant we will ever face will be the giant of doubt, specifically self-doubt. It seems as if every time we have a dream or an idea, there arises an equally powerful force that begins to not only contradict that dream but to assault it to the point of death. The giant of doubt is never easy to overcome, and the truth is that most people never truly overcome it at all.

What if there was a way to overcome the giants we face? What if there were some sort of formula or a powerful outside force that could give us a sizeable advantage and the ability to conquer a giant? The truth is that there are people—a lot of people—who have defeated their giant or giants, and are now living a life that is completely "giant-free."

Giants don't die easily. Historically, giants struck fear in the hearts of the people who lived in their areas. The Bible makes mention of them and their origin all the way back in Genesis:

> Now it came to pass, when men began to multiply on the face of the earth, and daughters were born to them, that the sons of God saw the daughters of men, that they were beautiful; and they took wives for themselves of all whom they chose. And the Lord said, "My Spirit shall not strive with man forever, for he is indeed flesh; yet his days shall be one hundred and twenty years." There were giants on the earth in those days, and also afterward, when the sons of God came in to the daughters of men and they bore children to them. Those were the mighty men who were of old, men of renown. Then the Lord saw that the wickedness

of man was great in the earth, and that every
intent of the thoughts of his heart was only evil
continually. And the Lord was sorry that He had
made man on the earth, and He was grieved in His
heart (Genesis 6:1-6).

Here we find some interesting insights. First, giants
were born as a result of fallen angels who had relations
with the people of the earth. These perverted and sinful
relationships gave birth to mighty men who were strong
in physical stature, but were known for their wickedness
and evil intent. We also see that God was grieved as a
result of the sin and literally mourned the fact that He
had made man on the earth. This was the origin of the
giants—and this would certainly not be the last we
hear of them.

There are many things in life that are difficult,
but there are others that seem nearly impossible to
accomplish. Anxiety assaults us at the very thought of
trying to do them. Throughout my life, I've seen people
struggling with different issues that they've fought very
hard to overcome. I've seen some struggle with being
overweight, fear, financial adversity, as well as health
issues or drug addiction. All of those who have been
successful in defeating these things have shared one
characteristic: persistence.

The Underdog

In my last book, *The Left-Handed Warrior*, I wrote
about an unlikely biblical hero by the name of Ehud. This

man did the impossible with the odds stacked heavily against him. He would never have been successful and brought about the national deliverance of his people if he had quit when things got difficult. For the successful, it seems as if adversity almost fuels their persistence. The harder the objective, the more of a challenge they perceive it to be. Refusing to be defeated and refusing to quit until you win will always be key in defeating the giants in your life.

For the successful, it seems as if adversity almost fuels their persistence.

When my oldest son, James, was just a little guy, he had a burning desire to play tackle football in the city youth league. When you watch football on television, you get the benefit of being able to live through the players without the pain they experience in the game. Little did my son know that actually playing the game would prove to be quite a bit more challenging than watching it on a Sunday afternoon. I took him to practice in the blazing Florida heat each day as these little guys trained and conditioned for several hours a day. My son was on the younger end of the age grouping he was placed in, and his only experience was in the backyard throwing around the football with me.

Things went pretty well for him and he kept up his excitement and motivation for the first couple of weeks. The objective of the coaching staff was to physically

Chapter 1: Hard to Kill

condition the kids before they got their pads and began hitting. When the first day of full-speed hitting came, James was excited but had no idea what to expect. I remember telling him what I could remember of my own football glory days, but that had been a couple of decades ago. He strapped up on that practice day and took the field with the rest of the kids to begin the various drills designed to teach kids the proper fundamentals of blocking and tackling.

I distinctly remember his first hit, and I'm pretty sure he does too. It was against a kid who was much bigger and older and had already been playing for some time. My son held his own, but I remember him looking at me after that first hit—and his face said it all. He didn't realize how hard that hit would be, and didn't realize the pain he would have to endure to be a football player.

During the drive home, we had a serious discussion about football and his future in the game. He was a little reluctant about continuing, and definitely didn't like hitting at all. I encouraged him and told him it would get better in time, but he would have to lose his fear of hitting in order to be successful. Each day I watched him play. It seemed like he tensed up and braced himself every time he collided with another player. His fear of injury was actually creating a higher likelihood of getting hurt.

Much like the first day of full pads, a day about three or four weeks into practice is seared into my memory—the day that James began to deliver a hit instead of remaining the target of someone else's hit.

Something just seemed to click; it was like he flipped an internal switch and lost his fear altogether. He lined up against one of his larger teammates, but this time, instead of cowering a bit before they collided, he actually extended his body and delivered a big hit. The other kid went flying backwards and landed on the ground. I was standing there with my mouth wide open. I felt bad for the kid but was admittedly very proud of my son! After that play, I watched him hit drill after drill. Now the fearful, tensed-up, timid player was gone. The other coaches began commenting to each other and me about the "new kid" on the football team. James had a great season and went on to excel in football, playing several years of city league and into high school. Why? He had overcome the giant of fear.

Success is often born at the
threshold of failure.

There was a time when he wanted to quit. But I knew that this was a much bigger issue than just a kid playing a childhood sport. There was a life lesson to be learned here; success is often born at the threshold of failure. Some giants are not defeated because their strength is too great. Some go unbeaten because we lack the persistence to keep fighting them. One of the most important keys to defeating your giant is the ability to stay focused and not quit.

Chapter 1: Hard to Kill

How It All Started

To really understand how to defeat the giants opposing you in your life, it is necessary to look back into the history of how they came into being. We have already seen their first mention in the Bible, but we do have some additional insight that gives us a deeper look into how complex of a problem they can be. In Numbers 13, a particular family line is identified as giants.

> And they went up through the South and came to Hebron; Ahiman, Sheshai, and Talmai, the descendants of Anak, were there (Now Hebron was built seven years before Zoan in Egypt.) (Numbers 13:22).

Not much is said about Anak in the Bible. We do know that he was a Canaanite and had three sons: Ahiman, Sheshai, and Talmai. Interestingly enough, the name Anak means, "a collar or an ornament."[1] This same name has shades of meaning that also reflect a long neck, or a long body, thus the race of giants that are connected to this name. I am always fascinated by peoples' names in the Bible and how much they correspond with the personality or achievements of that person. Many of the biblical names prove to be prophetic and show the hand of God in the naming of the child. There are also several examples of adults whose names were changed as God was trying to set them on a different path.

---

1. James Strong, "Lexicon: Strong's H6059 - anaq or Anak," Blue Letter Bible, accessed February 7, 2020, https://www.blueletterbible.org/lang/lexicon/lexicon.cfm?Strongs=H6059&t=KJV.

kill the giant.

Anak (collar or ornament) is also used to describe a yoke, like the ones oxen wore when plowing the fields. Oxen would be "collared" or yoked together to keep them in unison and lessen the likelihood of one of the animals straying from their appointed task. This neck collar, or yoke, proved to be an important piece of equipment because it would turn two separate animals into one single-working unit. This solitary unit was strong, single-minded, and stayed much more focused than a lone animal with no physical restraint.

If a farmer attempted to pull his plow with unyoked oxen, the results would be disastrous, even dangerous. The yoke was a staple item in the barn of every farmer; and without it, plowing became a slow and frustrating task. As we look at the name *Anak*, it is easy to see that the meaning of his name had symbolism for what his descendants would become, and for those who would resist them as well.

The three sons of Anak continued to reproduce and their offspring came to be known as the Anakim. These large and brutal men became a yoke on the necks of the people of Israel. This was not a yoke that created a well-defined, God-ordained purpose. Instead, it was a strong attachment to fear and disobedience. This yoke would become so strong, in fact, that an entire nation's future would be put on hold as a result of the fear that this family line of giants produced.

These giant warriors who were motivated by greed and evil were not easily defeated. The Anakim were

30

Chapter 1: Hard to Kill

known as vicious warriors and because of their size and strength they proved themselves to be hard to kill. Many stories have been written and told of the exploits of these men and the atrocities they doled out on their innocent victims.

Much like the giants of old, we too can be yoked together with things that seem to be impossible to defeat. As a pastor, I often speak with people who are dealing with issues they feel they cannot overcome. The reality is that the difficulty isn't just the magnitude of the problem, but the feeling of being yoked together with that problem and having no foreseeable way of breaking free from it. Like the yoke around the oxen's neck, we can become entangled and joined to our problems without any sense of hope of ever walking in freedom again.

The ministry of Jesus was designed to set people free. He released demoniacs, healed the sick, and even raised the dead. Situations that seemed sure to end in unavoidable failure were instantly turned around as Jesus set the captives free. The destiny of people's lives was truly changed, not just from physical bondage, but also from spiritual bondage.

The book of John tells us the riveting story of a woman who was caught breaking the Law of Moses. This wasn't a simple oversight involving religious handwashing or forgetting to pay a temple tax; no, this was a big one! This woman was actually caught in the very act of committing adultery. Not only was this humiliating and demoralizing, but it was punishable by death.

kill the giant.

> Now early in the morning He came again into
> the temple, and all the people came to Him; and
> He sat down and taught them. Then the scribes
> and Pharisees brought to Him a woman caught
> in adultery. And when they had set her in the
> midst, they said to Him, "Teacher, this woman was
> caught in adultery, in the very act. Now Moses, in
> the law, commanded us that such should be stoned.
> But what do You say?" (John 8:2-5).

Jesus had been teaching on forgiveness, and as
such, He had challenged some of the religious law that
had become the center of Jewish culture. When the
religious leaders caught this woman in her sin, they
immediately drug her to the feet of Jesus. They then
arrogantly reminded Jesus of the severity of this sin,
which was punishable by death, and asked what His
recommendation for her punishment would be. They
stood by, stones in hand, ready to execute the Law to the
fullest extent. They felt completely justified in taking the
life of this woman because she had the audacity to live
her life in such a despicable show of filth and flagrant
disregard of the Law.

Jesus' response was unforgettable and shocked the
religious leaders to their core. However, in His response,
Jesus revealed His ability as the ultimate Bondage
Breaker and Healer of sinful affliction.

> So when they continued asking Him, He raised
> Himself up and said to them, "He who is without
> sin among you, let him throw a stone at her first"
> (John 8:7).

Chapter 1: Hard to Kill

Silence permeated the air; nobody said a word. They were absolutely speechless! I'm sure this was a surprise to everyone, as the religious leaders were seldom without some sort of complicated and pretentious response. One after another the men began to drop their stones as they realized that they, too, were people riddled with inescapable sin.

Jesus then uttered these healing words to the humiliated and shamed woman, "Neither do I condemn you; go and sin no more." Notice that Jesus addressed the fact that what she did was actual sin ("go and sin no more") but offered what the Law could not—He offered the lack of guilt and shame. With these simple words, the yoke of oppressive religious law was shattered. This woman's family would not have to attend a funeral for a shamed and shunned woman who society would deem as deserving of death.

Now the attention of Jesus would move beyond the woman and to those who were so consumed with destroying her. Keep in mind that they were not only focused on executing her, but they felt completely justified in doing so. After some interaction based on Jesus' challenge of the worldview of the religious leaders, He made another statement. This declaration went beyond any argumentative dialogue and revealed the true heart and intent of Jesus' ministry. It would stand the test of time and prove itself to be true in many ways.

> Therefore if the Son makes you free, you shall be free indeed (John 8:36).

kill the giant.

This is what Jesus came to do; this is what the world truly needed but didn't even realize yet. Jesus came to extend God's freedom to humanity, and not just a fleeting feel-good type of freedom. He came to bring a *true* freedom that would transcend the physical realm and move into the spiritual realm. This woman's life wasn't only extended; it was changed forever. Jesus was telling her this: "Not only am I giving you a second chance, but I believe you can be successful. This is a fresh start for you, go and sin no more!"

Much like the bondage of sin and shame, the bondage produced by giants was not easy to overcome (these men were very hard to kill). Our own personal giant can take the form of addictions, depression, hurt, rejection, and on and on—and they can also be very hard to kill. These issues will never just resolve themselves. They will never fade away with time. These areas will have to be addressed and must have a spiritual component in order to be truly successful.

God's power can overcome what we don't have the ability to overcome on our own. People who have strong addictions need something that goes beyond psychology or self-help motivation; they need the same Jesus who set the adulterous woman free to set them free too. Scripture teaches that the anointing of God doesn't simply minimize the power of the yoke of bondage, but literally shatters the yoke so it no longer exists.

It shall come to pass in that day that his burden will be taken away from your shoulder, and his yoke

Chapter 1: Hard to Kill

from your neck, and the yoke will be destroyed
because of the anointing oil (Isaiah 10:27).

Now before all the theologians begin to correct me
on this, I do realize that this Scripture refers to the
nation of Israel and has implications of war and national
deliverance from the stronghold of Assyria. However,
the underlying principle here is the same: God's
powerful anointing can do more than we could ever do
on our own. In this specific case, God was showing that
He could do more than the entire army of trained Israeli
warriors. A quick study of history will prove that God
did, in fact, set the Hebrew people free from the bondage
of the Assyrians and set them up for continued victory in
the future. He can help us in the same way today.

> Any obstacle we face in life will
> usually appear much bigger than
> it actually is.

Much of the success the giants enjoyed was due to
their ability to intimidate those they were bullying. The
sheer size of a giant makes a clear statement: "I'm not
going down easy!" When you read the story of David
and Goliath, the Bible is very precise on the size of
Goliath and even the size of his weaponry. Why is this
even mentioned? The writer could not ignore what he
saw and heard. Any obstacle we face in life will usually
appear much bigger than it actually is.

The Intimidation Factor

One day our dishwasher stopped cleaning the top rack of dishes. We had to move the dirty dishes down to the bottom rack and rewash them, sometimes more than once, in order to get them clean. This went on for quite some time until my wife, Michelle, had enough. She said, "You have to either fix this dishwasher or I'm going to call a repair man." I didn't know anything about dishwasher repair, but I certainly didn't like the thought of paying a lot of money to someone else for a costly repair. I did a quick Internet search and discovered that the likely problem was in a small compartment in the bottom of the dishwasher which had some gears that were probably jammed and no longer turning properly.

I don't consider myself to be overly handy, but I have done some minor repair work around the house. Since I had no experience with fixing dishwashers, I could envision my attempt going wrong in any number of ways. I have to be honest and say that it was a bit overwhelming when I began to think about partially disassembling a dishwasher. I procrastinated as long as I could and even considered calling a repair company. However, after a long internal struggle, I finally decided to give it a try. Armed with some fresh tutorial videos I found online, I gathered the necessary tools and began my challenge.

As I started turning a few screws and removing a few inconspicuous parts, I quickly realized that the job was much simpler than I had imagined. In fact, it turned out

Chapter 1: Hard to Kill

to be something an average second grader could have done with very little support! Within a few minutes the dishwasher was up and running again. It was a great day. My wife was happy and the bonus was that she thought I was an incredible repair man. The take-a-way here? Many times we build things up to be much bigger and more difficult than they actually are. Had I never been pushed to try and fix that appliance, it would likely still be underperforming to this very day!

The idea of having to fight can
be overwhelming.

The greatest tool the giant possesses is the ability to intimidate and cause fear. Like the dishwasher repair job, some of the challenges we face are really not as difficult as we imagine them to be, but the idea of having to fight can be overwhelming. Many times, just a simple conversation with someone who isn't as emotionally involved as you are can help you gain a better perspective. When I speak with someone wiser and more experienced than I am, it helps me see things from a slightly less overwhelmed state of mind.

The intimidation factor can be very dangerous as it can rob you of your motivation. Few get motivated to embark on a contest they are sure to lose. Know that even though the giants didn't die easily, they were able to be defeated. In fact, not only did individual giants die, but the entire line of Anakim became extinct. This wasn't because they died of natural causes either. This

kill the giant.

happened because someone refused to be intimidated and took on the big challenge of eradicating them. We'll take a deeper look into this soon, but for now, understand that the actual Anakim, and the giants of your life are truly hard to kill, but *can be defeated*.

The Reality of the Giant

This book is supposed to be a motivational and equipping push for you. I wish I could tell you that you will never face any giants. I wish I could say that life will always be easy and you will never be challenged. I wish that everything in life always had a happy ending and you will never face any giants. But I can't say any of those things and remain truthful. I can tell you that the difficulties you face will seldom just disappear on their own; the giants in your life are too comfortable in their roles as intimidating and undefeated forces.

At the start of this chapter I shared about the "all-too-difficult-to-kill" weed. To eradicate the weed is seemingly impossible, but with continuous and dedicated diligence, weeds can be brought under control. My yard certainly isn't weed-free. However, there are very few weeds because I take the time to pull them in order to keep them under control. We can never remove all of the problems from our lives, but our persistence certainly pays off if we refuse to allow each and every situation to throw us into yet another emotional tailspin. It's time to kill your giant; it's time to trust God and walk hand in hand with Him as He helps you defeat the thing that is defeating you.

1: Hard to Kill
Action Points

Persistence Is Key: Pinpoint a few areas in your life in which you have not been consistent. Determine this in your heart from this point forward: "I will do my best to stay committed to this until I see the improvement I am shooting for." Sometimes the winners in life are not the best or most talented, but simply the ones who survive the longest. They keep at it. I heard a joke about two men walking in the woods.

> When they heard that they were in bear territory, one hunter said to the other, "What are we going to do if we are chased by a bear?"
>
> The other hunter responded, "I'll run as fast as I can."
>
> The first hunter answered back, "You can't outrun a bear."
>
> With that the other hunter responded, "I don't have to. I just have to outrun you!"

It's not always about being the best; sometimes it's about being the most dedicated.

Work Hard: Find some ways that you can apply yourself more diligently to the areas in which you are trying to excel. What can you do that will allow you to work even harder? Can you get up an hour earlier? Can you stay up an hour later? Is there a "time-waster" in your life that you can cut out? If you want to get what nobody else has got, then you have to do what nobody else has done. Remember, the giants didn't just die from old age; somebody was willing to face the challenge to stop this continual cycle of evil. My grandfather always told me, "The world owes you nothing." If you're waiting for your dreams to just fall in your lap, most likely you will be waiting an awfully long time and be sorely disappointed. In my life, I have always tried to be the hardest working person in the room. This is not a pride thing. It's more about understanding a vital key to success. What you are unwilling to work for, you will probably never achieve.

If you want to get what nobody else has got, then you have to do what nobody else has done.

Expect Adversity: Don't allow any push back to stop you in your tracks. If something resists you, that just means you're moving in the right direction. If nothing ever resists you, then you're not pushing hard enough. Instead of allowing yourself to become discouraged because of obstacles and adversity, let them serve as a reminder that resistance builds strength. Problems are not necessarily an indicator that you are on the wrong track; they simply mean that you've chosen a track that may be worth fighting for. I always tell our church, "If the Devil's not fighting against you, it's because he doesn't

Just like resistance training

see you as a threat!" Stand against adversity and refuse to let it quantify your faith.

Resistance builds strength.

Pray and Pray Again: Always remember, you are a force to be reckoned with, but at the end of the day, we are imperfect people. As we pray, it creates a stronger dependence on the Lord and less confidence in our own flesh. The true key to David's success did not come from the fact that he was a warrior-king; he was a warrior-king because of his faith in the Lord. When David was chosen, he met the criteria that God had spoken to the prophet who was given the task of anointing the next king.

> The Lord has sought for Himself a man after His own heart, and the Lord has commanded him to be commander over His people (1 Samuel 13:14).

David was a man of worship and prayer. The Psalms are filled with examples of David's prayers to God and his belief that God would vindicate him, even in the toughest of circumstances.

Refuse to Be Intimidated: Think of something new you can try in order to expand your arsenal of talent. Learn something from someone else; stop simply wishing that you could do certain things—and step out and give it a try. Watch someone who is a master of their craft; they tend to make what they do appear simple. Swapping out a car engine or building a house certainly isn't easy; unless you have already had success at doing it before.

kill the giant.

Sometimes we look at the obstacle in front of us and are too quick to think it's too difficult to overcome. The truth is, it probably isn't going to be easy, but that doesn't mean it's impossible. I'm not good at mechanics or building things, but with the right motivation and the need, I could learn how to do both of these things with some degree of success. It wouldn't be because I have experience, but because I had a hunger to learn. Never look at hard things and psych yourself out by believing you can never do them. Intimidation is a powerful adversary, but the only power it has over you is that which you allow. You can learn almost anything with the right instruction and dedication coupled with perseverance. Do not allow yourself to quit before you even test your ability through trying.

Dedication = strong support or loyalty to something or someone.

Perseverance = continuing in a course of action without regard to discouragement, opposition or previous failure.

Chapter 2:
Believe in You!

I 'll never forget the first time I ever spoke in public. Outside of my required Public Speaking class in high school, I had managed to be very successful in avoiding speaking to large groups of people. As countless surveys on fear have taught us, one of the most dominant fears that people have is public speaking. For me, this was certainly the case. In fact, the very thought of standing in front of even a small group was terrifying to me. I became so nervous that I would sweat, feel nauseous, and get a headache.

My wife and I were young newlyweds and someone from our church felt that God was leading them to pay for us to go on the church mission trip to South America. We went to help out and work where needed, but as far as doing anything in front of a crowd, we didn't really feel like that was our calling. Our plan was to work behind the scenes, preparing the items needed for our outreaches, and doing whatever additional legwork might be necessary to have a successful trip. Everything went pretty much as planned until about three days into the trip when I was approached by one of the youth pastors leading the trip. As my wife and I were a young married couple, the leaders felt we should have some additional responsibility. The youth pastor asked me to share my testimony at the church service that night.

As soon as the words flowed out of his mouth, my whole world went completely dark. My greatest fear was now being exposed, and to make matters even worse, it was right in front of my wife! To say that I was terrified or traumatized would be a gross understatement. I was so frightened, in fact, that when he posed the question, I just stood there and said nothing for what seemed like an eternity. I stood in awkward silence for so long that the youth pastor asked the question a second time. He followed up with the classic question, "Are you all right?" I was able to get it together enough to respond with the word *yes*, to which he said, "Great, I'll get with you more about this later this afternoon." I was actually saying yes to the "Are you all right?" question, not the "Will you share your testimony at the service tonight?" question!

As he walked away, my wife said to me, "I'm so proud of you for this." I stood there thinking to myself: *What just happened? Now it's too late to say no and my wife is telling me about how proud she is.* This was the perfect storm, the storm of total humiliation! I couldn't eat the rest of the day and couldn't stop trying to figure out what I was supposed to say or how I was supposed to stand up in front of an entire church full of people and talk to them.

Chapter 2: Believe in You!

My youth pastor (not the one who asked me to speak) could see that I was a little shaken. He began to share with me that God had set this trip up and that His intent was to stretch me. The Lord wouldn't want me to go on a trip like this and come back home without having been radically changed. He continued to share that he really saw potential in me and believed that I would do well sharing in front of the church that night.

I decided that I would go ahead and follow through with my commitment, even though it was technically made under duress. I managed to calm my nerves by telling myself that this would probably be a small church and poorly attended since this was summer and all. All afternoon I rehearsed what I would say that night at the church over and over. I even shared my testimony while looking at myself in the mirror. I practiced out on the balcony of our hotel room and while taking a shower before the service. I finally got to the point where I felt as if my preparation was as good as it was going to get. My testimony is one that may lack some of the flair that others have: It contained no drug addictions or jail time; but even so, God had brought me a long way. I was confident that in spite of my nerves, God could take my simple testimony and use it to reach people.

We got dressed and headed for the church. The bus ride over was filled with the regular instruction for the night of ministry and a few logistical details for the team. The youth pastor in charge that night shared that I would be the one sharing my testimony at the service.

kill the giant.

When he said my name, the people on the bus began to clap and cheer, and the butterflies in my stomach began to swarm. I was so nervous that I was actually nervous about being nervous!

As we pulled into the church parking lot I realized that this church was much bigger than I had hoped. We walked through the parking lot and then proceeded into the building. People were already beginning to fill the sanctuary, and we were about thirty minutes early. This was going to be more of a challenge than I'd anticipated. The service started, and what a service it was! We had an incredible time of worship; then some of our skits were performed, there were a few introductions, and then it was time for the testimony.

From the time my name was called until I walked off the stage still remains somewhat of a blur to me. I remember trying to share the same way I had while practicing in the mirror, but for some reason, I was talking fast—really fast. I managed to get through the testimony, and the people responded politely; in fact they were a little excessive in their response. As I sat down, one of the youth pastors came to me and said, "Wow, man, you are a natural in front of people." I sort of laughed. (I enjoy sarcasm as much as the next guy.) But then he said, "No, really, I think God has a call on your life to preach."

But over the next several weeks, God began to stir my wife and myself regarding a potential call to ministry. The words this man spoke to me kept ringing in my ear, not that I mistook his voice as God's call over me, but

Chapter 2: Believe in You!

he did encourage me to consider that possibility. To this day, that man probably doesn't realize the impact of his positive words to me on that day. His words were more than simple encouragement; they caused to me think differently. I began to think differently about the possibilities of my life; but more importantly, I began to think differently about the way I saw myself.

The way we see ourselves is critically important to our success in life. Think about it: If you wholeheartedly believed that you would fail if you attempted a certain task, most likely you wouldn't attempt it at all. Why would you put yourself through the pain of trying something in which you had no chance of success? On the other hand, if you really believed you could be successful at something— even if it was hard—you would stand a much better chance of attempting that task simply because you viewed the risk factor much more favorably.

What you see yourself becoming
in life is most likely what you
will become.

I am convinced that most people live their lives far beneath their true potential, not because they are only capable of average, but because they see themselves as only capable of average. What you see yourself capable of doing is most likely what you will end up doing. What you see yourself becoming in life is most likely what you will become. When I spoke to that church, I wasn't a public speaker at all, but that opportunity changed my way of thinking. Even though I wasn't a great speaker, by any means, the way I viewed myself began to change and it created the possibility of becoming something more than I had imagined before that time.

The giant of self-doubt and insecurity is intimidating and hard to defeat. This giant's greatest asset is the persona they have created. Most people in the days of the biblical giants had never seen a giant actually do battle. You would be hard-pressed to find more than a few biblical references to warfare involving a giant. The fear people had was created—not by seeing the giant in action for themselves—but by the words that came from other people. The giants, though large and intimidating, may not have been as great on the battlefield as many assume. Maybe they were slow or maybe they weren't mentally acute or aware of their surroundings. Few people were willing to even try to defeat them, so the legend of their strength and skill in combat went unchallenged, and thus grew out of proportion with reality.

> Any time you prepare to take on your giant, know that a flood of criticism is sure to ensue.

One of the descendants of the Anakim, Goliath from Gath, was also unchallenged. In this prominent biblical story, the giant's reputation of strength went far beyond the borders of his home country of Philistia. The fear of Goliath was a result of his size and his apparent reputation. A young shepherd boy by the name of David volunteered to fight the giant, but his faith was quickly attacked by those positioned around him. Any time you prepare to take on your giant, know that a flood of criticism is sure to ensue. In fact, as you look deeper into the story you will realize that some of David's harshest criticism came from those who were closest to him.

The story began with David simply being obedient to his father to carry some supplies to his three brothers who were Hebrew soldiers at war with the Philistines. The unassuming young man quickly realized that things weren't going so well for the Hebrews. The giant was coming out twice a day and bellowing his loud, obnoxious threats in the valley that separated the two armies. His voice echoed for miles as the sound waves carried through the valley and bounced off the mountains. Fear had eclipsed the soldiers to the point of paralysis, but David stood unshaken. As he began to inquire about the situation, David was quickly chastised by his own brother.

> Now Eliab his oldest brother heard when he spoke to the men; and Eliab's anger was aroused against David, and he said, "Why did you come down here? And with whom have you left those few sheep in the wilderness? I know your pride and the insolence of your heart, for you have come down to see the battle" (1 Samuel 17:28).

Sometimes the people who are closest to us have the ability to hurt us the most. In most cases, I don't believe this is intentional, but nonetheless, it is still very true.

49

kill the giant.

The people we've walked with through trials, problems, and difficulties usually know us better than the average person. However, as the old saying goes, "familiarity breeds contempt." Sometimes people who know us very well, see us as the person we've always been, but lack the vision to see us as the person we are becoming.

Recently, I ran into my cousin who I had not seen in well over thirty years. In my last memory of her, she was a little girl. That image was locked into my mind from our childhood. When I saw her, I didn't even recognize her. In fact, I never would have known who she was had she not introduced herself. It was hard for me to see her as a grown woman with a husband, kids, and a career! People often predefine who we can become, what we can do, and how far we can go. They only do this because they gauge that thinking on what has been done in the past.

The failures you have had in
the past are no indicator of
the potential victories in
your future.

When David's older brother saw him, he couldn't see the giant killer within him. He might have seen David as the obnoxious teenager he had always been before. He may have known him as the one who was always vying for their parent's attention, and possibly, as the younger brother, David may have been a tattletale. Whatever the reason, the past history between Eliab and David prevented Eliab from seeing what David could become.

Chapter 2: Believe in You!

In these situations, you must remember that the failures you have had in the past are no indicator of the potential victories in your future. Sometimes the people close to us have had an up-close and personal look at areas of our life in which we have been the most vulnerable. That mental image of our small mistakes, or even our bigger disasters, is locked into their minds and they may not be able to see beyond that. We have to be careful to not allow other people's perceptions to place restrictions around us and keep us from believing for more.

Never allow other's poor view of themselves to be placed upon you.

David could have listened to his older brother and thought to himself, "You know, he's right. Maybe I do have a pride problem. Maybe I am better suited to take care of sheep and leave the fighting to those who have been properly trained." If he would have allowed that thinking to affect him, he would have placed restraints on the very thing that God had called him to do. The real issue with Eliab was that he could not see himself defeating the giant, therefore he could not see his little brother defeating the giant either.

One of the issues we face with people is that many are quick to place their own insecurities and deficiencies on others. If I don't believe that I can be successful, it may be hard for me to believe that you can be successful. Eliab, whose faith could not be compared to David's,

kill the giant.

felt that he was no match for this bellowing giant. However, David's belief in God created a healthy sense of his own self-worth. Never allow other's poor view of themselves to be placed upon you. Just because they don't think themselves able to do something, doesn't mean that you have to embrace those same feelings about yourself.

It would be nice if that was the only obstacle of misplaced doubt that David had to face before squaring off with the giant. However, this was only the first. Next the young shepherd would have to convince King Saul that he was a worthy opponent for the giant. As we continue to read the story, we see that the word began to spread that there was an active challenger who was willing to fight the Philistine giant.

I wonder what Saul's reaction was when he heard that finally someone was willing to fight and a put an end to this humiliating display of military cowardice. The armies of Israel had been at a standstill for weeks; and due to their own fear, showed no promise of engaging any time soon. I imagine he was hopeful as he realized there was a challenger, and I believe he would have had some expectations about the would-be warrior. Saul probably expected a very large, muscular, rough, deep-voiced man that had proven himself to be successful in years of historical battle. This man would most likely have scars all over his body from wounds received from past battles, only to emerge as the victor time and again. He would be a disheveled man's man who was so fierce that he had little concern with personal hygiene, a man whose passion was taking down anyone who dared to defy him. Yet what Saul expected and what he saw were two very different things. The scriptural account shows us that Saul was less than enthusiastic about David's willingness to volunteer.

> "Don't be ridiculous!" Saul replied. "There's no way you can fight this Philistine and possibly win! You're only a boy, and he's been a man of war since his youth" (1 Samuel 17:33 NLT).

How many times do we let other
people define for us what
we can do?

Can you imagine what was running through Saul's mind? His expectation of a rough-cut soldier was now squashed by the introduction of a gangly teenager. Saul never questioned David about his experience in battle; he did not question him as to why he thought he had a chance against the giant. By what he saw, Saul immediately conferred upon David his thoughts of impossibility. He did not even say, "You most likely will not succeed"; he told the boy undeniably, "You are not able to do this." How many times do we let other people define for us what we can do?

In my last book, *The Left-Handed Warrior*, I extensively tell the story of a church we started in northern Florida. One of the pivotal moments from that experience was when I was told this by another pastor: "Several others have tried to start a church here before and were unsuccessful." When I say *pivotal*, it's because the statement he made became fuel for me when our venture became difficult. We could have allowed that remark to deter us, but either because we were young and foolish or because we were full of faith, that statement became a motivator instead.

Sometimes the negative words of another's assumptions can actually benefit your overall progress. When David was told "You can't" two times, he clearly recognized that this was in direct conflict with what he knew to be true. David knew that God's hand was on his life; he knew that God had shown Himself faithful before; and he knew his overall purpose wasn't complete. If we allow every remark that people make about our lives, our dreams, or our purpose to define our success, we will quit before we ever get started.

If we allow every remark that people make about our lives, our dreams, or our purpose to define our success, we will quit before we ever get started.

As Saul is giving his assessment on the validity of David's request, we have to realize that none of it is fact-based. His comment about David's lack of ability assumes an awful lot about a person he doesn't even know. Notice there is no real data quoted here. David's presumed inability is solely due to his age. There was no official ranking system or even a test to determine the skill level of a "would-be" fighter. This analysis of David was not based on credible information at all.

Most of the people who make judgments about your likelihood of success lack the credentials to make those assessments. I often cringe when I hear people tell kids things like, "You'll never be good at football because you're too small," or "You'll never be a good basketball player because you're too short." These statements usually come from people who are making that assessment by comparing these kids to the athletes they see on television. I don't know too many seven-foot eight-year-olds, so by that criteria, nobody would ever be successful.

The responsibility of the dream
rests on the dreamer.

There has to be a belief in one's self that is not based on someone else's vote before we move toward our dream. Remember, you have to believe in yourself in order to maintain the momentum to accomplish your dream. It is nice when others come alongside of your dream and speak life into you and believe in you as you advance, but truly successful people understand that the responsibility of the dream rests on the dreamer. David had an audacious dream—one that would lay his life on the line. In this story, nobody walked with David to accomplish his goal. Nobody encouraged him, and nobody believed in him. But that didn't stop David. He believed in himself because he believed in his God.

What if David would have accepted what Saul said? It would have been easy for David to have been discouraged and unwilling to fight based on the words of the king. After all, this was the king. He, better than anyone, would be qualified to determine what made a successful soldier. David could have easily just walked away. However, he was so sold out to his belief, and so determined about his dream that he refused to be intimidated by anyone—even the king himself!

> Stop hesitating in your purpose
> because you are waiting for
> others to push you.

David didn't require a vote of confidence; David chose to believe in himself. His passion for the dream was bigger than the opposition against the dream. If David's success depended on the constant push from others, he never would have stepped out on the battlefield that day. I want to encourage you, stop hesitating in your purpose because you are waiting for others to push you; allow the purpose itself to push you.

Most people have an innate desire to be liked. We appreciate a warm compliment or a confirmation that someone believes in us. Visionary leaders and big dreamers know this though; the bigger the dream we have, the more the opposition and enemies there will be to that dream. We have to be able to move past ridicule, naysayers, and people who are happy to function in a passive or negative environment. I can't let someone else's lack of faith and lack of spiritual aggression compromise my dream.

Most successful business people will tell you that they didn't get to the level of success they are currently in because everything was easy. In fact, many can share a history of failures, setbacks, and discouragements. The truth is, if becoming a millionaire was easy, most everyone would be one! Accomplishing your dream and fulfilling your destiny will never be a walk in the park; it will come with blood, sweat, and tears. But it is possible if you refuse to give up!

The giant's success was largely based on nothing more than intimidation. Goliath didn't kill a single person on the day of David's famous showdown. His perceived greatness and fierce reputation did not bring about his success that day. After it's all said and done, many of the threats against our success that seem so powerful and worthy of our concern, end up being little more than shallow words.

Many of the threats against our success that seem so powerful and worthy of our concern, end up being little more than shallow words.

This story reminds us of how God can take a small person with little proven success and cause them to be successful beyond their imagination. The truth was that this victory over the giant would pale in comparison to the victories destined for David's future. This once-untested shepherd boy would not only overcome giants, but entire armies, kingdoms, and other insurmountable odds.

Like the long handle of a lever, leverage is created when you believe in yourself. Like the small grain of mustard seed that Jesus referred to in the Gospels, your acknowledgment of who God made you to be has the potential to move mountain-sized obstacles.

> So Jesus said to them, "Because of your unbelief; for assuredly, I say to you, if you have faith as a mustard seed, you will say to this mountain, 'Move from here to there,' and it will move; and nothing will be impossible for you (Matthew 17:20).

This story comes after an unsuccessful prayer by the disciples for a young child who was demon possessed. Jesus gave this well-known response after their prayer yielded no results. Jesus blamed the lack of result on their unbelief. It belonged to them. Jesus said it happened because "of *your* (italics mine) unbelief." They needed to see themselves as God's mode of delivery for this young man's healing. The responsibility didn't belong to society, God, or anyone else; it was theirs.

We have to realize that our purpose is God-given; it doesn't come from us; it comes from Him. The assignment of the purpose is God's responsibility, but believing and acting upon that purpose is our responsibility. Just like the disciples who dropped the ball because they had

Chapter 2: Believe in You!

unbelief, we also fall short when we don't believe in ourselves. Our ability to grasp God's vision for our life and then truly see ourselves the way He sees us is crucial to our success. You want to talk about someone who really believed in themselves? Look at David's verbal response and challenge to Goliath when challenged by him on the field of battle:

> Then David said to the Philistine, "You come to me with a sword, with a spear, and with a javelin. But I come to you in the name of the Lord of hosts, the God of the armies of Israel, whom you have defied. This day the Lord will deliver you into my hand, and I will strike you and take your head from you. And this day I will give the carcasses of the camp of the Philistines to the birds of the air and the wild beasts of the earth, that all the earth may know that there is a God in Israel. Then all this assembly shall know that the Lord does not save with sword and spear; for the battle is the Lord's, and He will give you into our hands" (1 Samuel 17:45-47).

David was careful to give God all the glory and credit for his success, but he acknowledged his part in the battle too. David said: "This day the Lord will deliver you into *my* hand and *I* will strike you and take your head from you" (emphasis mine). As he continued in this brief exchange, it was obvious that David was no pushover; in fact, he was gutsy and full of faith!

As I write this, I can almost hear my critics begin to say, "This is just another positive-thinking book. We need nothing more than faith in God!" To those of this opinion, I would remind you of what is written by the apostle James concerning our faith:

> Thus also faith by itself, if it does not have works, is dead (James 2:17).

On the day of David's classic battle, the battlefield was filled with men of faith. The Hebrews were raised to be staunchly religious and to trust in the Lord. Though there were many men of faith, there was only one man of action; he came in the form of a young shepherd boy who dared to believe God and believe in himself. God has invested Himself in each of us; that investment is the very seed of the Almighty God. His seed was never designed for failure, but for success; and not just "getting by" success, but *outrageous giant-killing success*.

One thing we can count on for sure in this life is that we will always face giants. There will always be those who doubt our ability, and those who don't believe in us. Though those will always be present, there is also a God who is present, and He believes in you when others may have given up on you.

You can do more than you think you can; you know more than you realize; and you are better than people say that you are.

When I was a young and aspiring youth pastor, I was full of self-doubt. My own insecurities could have stopped, and even prevented, me from fulfilling the calling on my life. I am thankful today that God has helped me to begin to see myself in a different light. Although I have a long way to go yet, as most of us do, I am learning to see myself in a way that is closer to the way He sees me. You can do more than you think you can; you know more than you realize; and you are better than people say that you are.

As you continue reading this book, I want to challenge you. Don't read this like you've read other books, where you're trying to maybe find a few keys for personal growth that you can apply to your life. Although I hope that you do find some of those keys, I want to encourage to read this book through the eyes of a believer. Not only a believer in Christ, but a believer in you! As you read these remaining chapters, believe that these words aren't written for others, but for you. Believe in you, because God sure does!

2: Believe in You!
Action Points

Listen: Often others will see things in you that you don't see in yourself. Think back to the compliments others have given you, but you were quick to dismiss. Things like: "You are very good at..." or "You should start a business doing..." are good starting points. Write a list of those compliments and compile them for your own study. It just might be that your next big achievement has been hinted at numerous times in the past. In my life, someone else saw my public speaking gift before I did. Remember, you cannot gauge what you do on the basis of other's opinions; however, when trusted people speak into your life and they begin to call out the gifts and strengths within you, you would be wise to pay close attention. I believe that God brings people into our lives to build us and encourage our strengths as we are developing.

Don't Settle: Answer this question: "What is my next?" If you could do anything, what would it be? Would you drive for that big promotion, would you become an entrepreneur, would you go back to school? Start from the answer to that question and begin to sketch out a path to get there. The only person keeping you stuck in your current situation is *you*. If you settle for less, that is exactly what you will get: less! Whether it's that big promotion, new business venture, or fitness goal, never settle for less than you can accomplish. It's a sad thought, but I believe most people could have accomplished much more in their lifetimes had they only refused to settle. Never see yourself for where you are now, see yourself for where you are going. If you limit yourself to the now, you rob yourself of growth potential and future success. You were made for success and high potential.

Leave the Past behind You: Don't view your future through the lens of your past. Compile a list of major failures in your life. Take that list and thank God that He brought you through that and then thank Him that the past is over. Now, throw that list in the trash and decide that those things will never hold you back again. The failures of your past have no bearing on the success of your future. Thomas Edison's teachers reportedly said he was "too stupid to learn anything." He was fired from his first two jobs for being "non-productive." As an inventor, Edison made countless unsuccessful attempts at inventing the light bulb. When a reporter asked, "How did it feel to fail so many times?" Edison replied, "I have not failed. I've just found 10,000 ways that won't work." What if Edison had quit because of past failure? Always look forward and shake off the weight of past failure.

Use Your Advantages: Think through some of the victories you have had in your life. It may be landing that tough job, getting accepted by your college, or even your spouse accepting your proposal. Can you see the hand of God in those things? The reason you've been blessed to the degree you have is because you have a distinct advantage. You might be saying, "What advantage do I have?" You have the advantage of God's help working on your behalf to accomplish what you would be unable to do on your own. It is like when a frail, elderly woman without the strength to lift up a car uses a floor jack under its frame and pushes down on that long handle, giving her some leverage to lift her car. The muscles that couldn't move the car before, now move it with ease. The leverage creates an advantage that allows her to do more than she could do by herself.

> You have the advantage of God's help working on your behalf to accomplish what you would be unable to do on your own.

God, working on our behalf, causes us to be able to defeat the giants that oppose us and cause us to be successful in the things we couldn't do on our own. In the same way that God encouraged the Israelites when going out to battle against the Assyrians, God will go before you.

Be strong and courageous; do not be afraid nor dismayed before the king of Assyria, nor before all the multitude that is with him; for there are more with us than with him (2 Chronicles 32:7).

Chapter 3:
Defeating Doubt

When I was a boy we lived in a city in Florida which happened to be very close to a number of lakes. One of the activities that many people in our area participated in was water skiing. I can remember watching other people ski as I stood on the shore, thinking, *That looks like so much fun!* Eventually we made friends with some people who had a boat, and one of their weekend rituals was to take the family out and spend hours skiing around the lake. We were soon invited to tag along with them one Saturday, and some of the kids asked me if I wanted to give it a try. At first, I was hesitant, but then I decided to go ahead and give it a shot.

I remember strapping on those water skis and waiting intently to get pulled up by the boat and begin having the time of my life. As I held on to the rope, the boat begin to pull forward slowly as the ski rope tightened. As soon as it got tight, the boat began to accelerate in order to pull me up. Even though I had been told not to do this, a little panic set in and instead of leaning back I leaned forward—and my first ski experience ended in an embarrassing face plant. I tried several more times to get up on the skis, but only became more and more frustrated. If someone had been making a documentary called "How Not to Ski," each and every attempt would have been prime video footage. Finally, I climbed back in the boat, intent on watching the other (experienced) kids have a great time skiing.

Lap after lap they went until all of them were worn out. Someone said to me, "Hey, why don't you give it another try?" My first internal response was one of doubt and discouragement. I had already tried multiple times, unsuccessfully. Maybe I was just not made to ski. Maybe I should start looking for another recreational hobby.

After some words of encouragement and more technical pointers, out of the boat I went again. Even though I had failed multiple times, I was pretty determined to make this work. If for no other reason than I was tired of being embarrassed by a bunch of kids, many younger than me. I believed that this time it would be different. As the boat began to inch forward and the rope tightened, my stomach was full of butterflies. I knew this was it. The boat began to accelerate, and with great awareness of the latest instruction I had received, I concentrated on getting up and skiing. I heard the motor rev, and the rope became taut. The muscles in my arms and legs strained under the pressure, and for a moment I almost leaned sideways and fell. As I kept focusing though, I realized that I had not fallen, and in fact, I was now standing *and skiing* for the very first time! Amazing!

Chapter 3: Defeating Doubt

My own doubt almost prevented me from even attempting a feat in which I would find eventual success. If I would have quit that day, I would have missed out on hours upon hours of childhood fun, skiing around many of the lakes in our area. I would have been robbed of the countless memories I still have of skiing during the summers in those Florida lakes. Doubt is a menacing thief that can rob you of great potential in your life.

Doubt is not an emotion, a feeling, or an environment; doubt is a disease! Have you ever attempted to accomplish something that seemed bigger than your capabilities? Nagging feelings of doubt about your potential for success make that task much harder. Alternatively, when you enter a challenge with a sense of confidence, though not a guarantee of success, it certainly helps your odds.

Doubt is not an emotion, a feeling, or an environment; doubt is a disease!

Numerous studies have shown that when people really think they can succeed at something, they stand a much better chance of doing it well. These same studies show that when people are plagued with doubt or feelings of hopelessness concerning success, they stand a much higher chance of failing. From my own experience with people, I've noticed that when children were raised in a family in which their parents encouraged and promoted their overall success and value, these kids generally grow up to be successful and productive members of society. Kids who are raised in environments where they are met with constant negativity and reminders of their shortcomings have great struggles in adapting to life as adults.

Many sermons have been preached using the illustration of Roger Bannister. Before 1954 it was considered humanly impossible to run the mile in less than four minutes. For years, people had run and officially recorded their time in the mile, but no one had ever broken that barrier. People had resigned themselves to believing that no human could ever do better than breaking the five-minute mark. However, on May 6, 1954, Mr. Bannister ran a mile in three minutes and fifty-nine seconds.[2]

What's even more interesting is that since he broke that historic milestone in 1954, thousands of people have broken the once-thought-to-be-impossible four-minute barrier. What changed? What was it that has enabled countless people to do what was once thought impossible? With doubt removed and the absence of the word *impossible,* people have shattered that barrier time and time again.

When you doubt yourself, you automatically start off penalized. When you believe you can do something, you have already won a large part of the battle. Doubt

2. Frank Litsky and Bruce Weber, "Roger Bannister, First Athlete to Break the 4-Minute Mile, Dies at 88," The New York Times (The New York Times, March 5, 2018), http://www.nytimes.com/2018/03/04/obituaries/roger-bannister-dead.html)

Chapter 3: Defeating Doubt

is a weight hanging around the neck of the would-be dreamer or would-be record breaker. We all remember the children's story of the little train puffing up the hill. When the train began to believe it could succeed, its confidence in what it believed provided the momentum it needed to make it to the top. I believe you can make it to the top as well; but in order to do so, you first have to get rid of doubt.

Doubt is a weight hanging around the neck of the would-be dreamer or would-be record breaker.

I've had the pleasure of assisting as a coach as my kids grew up playing sports. It is always such a joy to watch these little boys and girls learn how to do things for the first time. When they catch their first pass playing football, score their first soccer goal, or make their first basket in basketball, they realize that they actually have some potential. I've watched as kids have shot baskets over and over with no success. You can almost script their reaction as you watch them become more and more frustrated. Sometimes their frustration leads them to the point of wanting to give up. As coaches, we encourage them to stick with it and keep trying. We know that if they can just get a little taste of success, it will motivate them to continue. Sure enough, when they finally get that ball in the hoop, it inspires them to get better and keep practicing.

kill the giant.

The game of life has a lot of similarities to sports. As a pastor, I've seen many people who are plagued with doubt. People can doubt all kinds of things: they doubt their success in life as a whole, they doubt the longevity of their marriage, they doubt their ability to be promoted in their jobs, and the list goes on. As long as people doubt themselves, it creates an imaginary boundary around the possibility of success. In contrast, when people believe they can succeed, it causes them to keep pushing, keep trying, and keep believing until they finally do succeed.

I am usually a fairly good judge of character. Often, part of my responsibility as a pastor is dealing with staffing our organization. As strange as it may sound, I can tell a lot about someone's attitude by the way they walk. Barring some sort of physical problem, a person's posture and the way they carry themselves is revealing. Once I hired a guy for our maintenance team, who I honestly had a lot of reservations about in the beginning. My concerns stemmed from the fact that he was a little older than our other guys. I wasn't sure if he would have the stamina to do the work, which was sometimes strenuous and physically demanding. When he walked in, he didn't walk with a hesitant or passive attitude; he walked like he intended to get somewhere, and get there fast! After spending only a few moments with him, my concerns were quickly relieved. I could see in his eyes and hear in his voice that he was a "go-getter."

The game-changer for me was his attitude. His age was the same after the interview as it was before; he didn't magically become any younger. I didn't have him demonstrate his physical abilities by lifting dumbbells, doing push-ups, or running on a treadmill. His attitude portrayed one of confidence, and his positive demeanor alleviated all of my concerns. He was able to quickly convince me that my reservations were unwarranted and that he could not only do the job, but exceed my expectations. This wasn't an act on his behalf. This was the actual mindset he had developed. He was truly confident and wasn't plagued by his own self-doubt. His positivity made me a believer!

Mighty David

We just read about young David and how he defeated the intimidating giant. We are all impressed by this powerful story of a young man, who, against all odds, stood toe-to-toe with that overgrown brute and defeated him with a single blow. However, as I read about David, I am equally impressed by his pitch to King Saul who had to give his permission for him to be the lone representative for the people of Israel.

What started as David performing a food delivery service to his brothers (soldiers in the battle), ended up proving to be a divine appointment set by God Himself. David was faithful to perform the request of his father and delivered bread and cheese to his hungry brothers. Once he arrived though, he realized that this would not be the normal "pop-in" visit to his brothers with a quick return to his regular mundane life. What would happen next would change the course of life, not only for David, but also for the future of a nation.

When David saw that the Philistine giant came and threatened the soldiers on a daily basis, something inside of him rose up, and said, "This isn't right." David knew that it wasn't fair nor was it the destiny of Israel to live in a constant state of fear and anxiety. Israel was not only being threatened by a rogue nation, they now had to deal with this rogue soldier in the form of a nasty giant.

> David refused to be deterred by people who could only see him for who he had been and not for what he would become.

David began to do some investigation and realized that there would be a pretty significant reward to the man who could defeat the giant. As he nosed around further, he was met with some significant opposition, much of which came from his oldest brother. Remember, his brother, Eliab, had known David from childhood. He knew his weaknesses, had seen his failures, and couldn't see him as anything beyond his kid brother. However, David refused to be deterred by people who could only see him for who he had been and not for what he would become.

Think about that for a minute. We are surrounded by people who lack the capacity to see our potential. Maybe it's the boss who thinks of us as nothing more than a simple "do-as-you're-told" employee. It could be your coworkers who can't see your potential because they're too busy trying

Chapter 3: Defeating Doubt

to create their own. People who are able to successfully defeat self-doubt have the ability to rise above the short-sighted viewpoints of others and believe in themselves.

Sometimes the nemesis of our self-confidence isn't people at all; sometimes it's the circumstances we face. We've all had things that seem to come up at exactly the wrong time. It seems like we're finally on the right track and then out of nowhere, a situation arises that threatens our hope of success. I have a poster that hangs in my office that I look at often; it is a constant reminder to me that success never comes easy and that the underdog can win against all odds. It's a quick snapshot of many years of a man's life, years filled with disappointment and pain. However, in the end, he rose to become one of the greatest presidents history has ever recorded.

Failed in business: claimed bankruptcy at age 22
Defeated in race for legislature at age 23
Failed in business: claimed bankruptcy at age 24
Lost love: fiancée dies at age 26
Nervous breakdown at age 27
Defeated in election at age 29
Defeated once again in election at age 31
Defeated for U.S. Congress at age 34
Defeated again for U.S. Congress at age 39
Defeated for U.S. Senate at age 46
Defeated for U.S. Vice-President at age 47
Defeated again for U.S. Senate at age 49

Abraham Lincoln was finally elected President of
the United States at age 51!

kill the giant.

Failure and defeat may seem like the theme of your life, but you cannot afford to embrace this as your identity. Every defeat is another layer of growth and a foundation to lead you to success. Nobody has ever gotten to the top of their field, career, sport, financial status, or any other area of success without some serious bumps and bruises along the way. In fact, most success stories have some major defeats listed in their résumé.

Most success stories have some major defeats listed in their résumé.

When David approached the battlefield that day to eventually face Goliath, he was not deterred by the negativity of his brother; in fact, I believe it actually motivated him. His mindset was probably, "If my brother is against this, I must be on to something." You have to appreciate the unspoken pecking order in the rivalry of brothers!

David had something special working within him. The hand of God was on his life and he had been specifically prepared for this moment—but there was something more. Just like David, we have also been specifically designed by God to accomplish things that only we can do. Many times, however, there is a distance between what we have the ability to do, and what we believe we have the ability do. For David, this distance was narrowed by his belief in himself.

Chapter 3: Defeating Doubt

David believed so strongly that he could defeat the giant that he was even able to convince King Saul to allow him to fight. In those days, when two champions faced off against each other, they did so as representatives of their nation. For the king to allow David to fight meant that he would have to have a great deal of trust in the young man. This was not simply a contest between two men, *but a contest between two nations*. At first King Saul wasn't on David's side.

> Now when the words which David spoke were heard, they reported them to Saul; and he sent for him. Then David said to Saul, "Let no man's heart fail because of him; your servant will go and fight with this Philistine." And Saul said to David, "You are not able to go against this Philistine to fight with him; for you are a youth, and he a man of war from his youth." But David said to Saul, "Your servant used to keep his father's sheep, and when a lion or a bear came and took a lamb out of the flock, I went out after it and struck it, and delivered the lamb from its mouth; and when it arose against me, I caught it by its beard, and struck and killed it. Your servant has killed both lion and bear; and this uncircumcised Philistine will be like one of them, seeing he has defied the armies of the living God." Moreover David said, "The Lord, who delivered me from the paw of the lion and from the paw of the bear, He will deliver me from the hand of this Philistine." And Saul said to David, "Go, and the Lord be with you!" (1 Samuel 17:31-37).

kill the giant.

It is clear that David believed in himself. I often say this: "If you don't believe in yourself, then nobody else will believe in you either." How did David do this? How could he believe that he had the capacity to do something he had never done before? It wasn't as if David had ever killed a giant before. It would have been different if he had carried a long list of defeated foes written on blood-stained papyrus scrolls in his back pocket. However, that wasn't the case. David carried only a strong faith and trust that God would give him victory.

If you don't believe in yourself, then nobody else will believe in you either.

David's self-confidence was so prevalent that it was contagious. Why do I say that? Even the king, who had everything to lose, believed that David could defeat the giant. David was so full of faith and self-confidence that in just three powerful sentences David transformed Saul from a "doubter" to a "defender"! Saul went from a man of fear to a man of faith with only three simple statements. Let's look at the ways David defeated doubt.

3: Defeating Doubt
Action Points

David demonstrated at least five keys to defeating doubt that we can learn from.

Do Not Let Your Past Define You

David refused to be defined by his past. His oldest brother remembered him as the young, annoying, incapable, adolescent boy. Eliab could not see him as a mighty warrior because his perception of David was limited by his own experience. In Eliab's eyes, David was a young shepherd boy, and to him, he would never amount to anything more than that.

There is a difference between letting your past teach you and letting your past define you.

Say these words out loud: "My past will not define me."

Everyone reading these words has some sort of a past. For many, it may be mostly positive, but chances are, there are probably a few things hiding in us of which we aren't proud, things which we are not keen to discuss. Our past is important because it gives us a historical background to all that God has brought us through. Hopefully, we've all learned some things from our own mistakes, and with the wisdom of past consequences, we make better choices now.

77

Having said that though, there is a difference between letting your past teach you and letting your past define you. I've learned a lot by my past poor choices, but I refuse to be characterized, defined, or stopped because of them. When we were babies, the only way we could move around was to crawl; we didn't have the coordination or muscle strength to walk upright. As we began to get older, stronger, and more experienced we began to pull up on furniture and then eventually, we gained the leg and back strength to walk. Were it not for the experience of crawling, we may have never developed the ability to walk. We didn't continue crawling forever, as crawling didn't define us. Crawling is what we used to do before gaining the experience to do more.

Never allow the person you used to be gain control over the person you want to be!

We have to see the teaching value held in past experience, but we also have to move beyond it into new territory. It is true that David was only an inexperienced shepherd, but he refused to allow his past to create his future. Never allow the person you used to be gain control over the person you want to be!

Handle Criticism Correctly

David did not allow criticism to change who he knew he was. Doing this helped him defeat his self-doubt. We've all been pierced by the verbal darts of well-intentioned people, who in an effort to "help us," criticize in a not-so-helpful way. If we are not careful, we will allow the words of a few to be louder than the words of the many.

As a pastor, I know all too well the endless land mines of potential controversy when dealing with people. The number of opinions are determined by the number of people in the room: one for each of them. Everyone has an opinion; some of them are helpful and some of them can be hurtful or just plain destructive.

The next time you see your
enemies, shake their hand. They
played a large role in helping
you become the person you
are today!

There are times when you need to make a decision based upon what you feel the leading of the Lord is. There will be people who misunderstand you and disagree, but at the end of the day, you have to be all right with that and still do the right thing. The criticism David heard could have crippled him and plagued him with so much self-doubt that Israel would have lost the battle. However, he refused to allow any criticism to change his purpose and what he knew God was empowering him to do.

I want to challenge you with this: when you are confident of your actions, absolutely refuse to give ear to those who offer critical advice. When people are critical of you, it can actually help you to better formulate what you really stand for. If nobody ever challenged you, you would have no real reason to take a stand. Sometimes your enemies are the greatest growth factors in your life. David's negative brother helped him define his boldness and take a stand against the giant nobody else was willing to face. The next time you see your enemies, shake their hand. They played a large role in helping you become the person you are today!

Refuse to Be Intimidated

David didn't allow the size of his challenge to intimidate him. When you read the story leading up to the classic battle between the young man and the giant, you will notice that a lot of attention is placed on the size of the giant. The author relates Goliath's physical height as well as the size of his weaponry.

> And a champion went out from the camp of the Philistines, named Goliath, from Gath, whose height was six cubits and a span. He had a bronze helmet on his head, and he was armed with a coat of mail, and the weight of the coat was five thousand shekels of bronze. And he had bronze armor on his legs and a bronze javelin between his shoulders. Now the staff of his spear was like a weaver's beam, and his iron spearhead weighed six hundred shekels; and a shield-bearer went before him (1 Samuel 17:4-7).

It is apparent that even the author was pretty impressed with the size and strength of the giant. I don't believe these details are here because the author was intimidated, but for the reader to better understand the depth of the miracle that was beginning to take shape.

The giant of self-doubt in your life will always portray itself to be much stronger than it actually is. The truth was that this particular giant was only a stone's throw away from defeat. It just required the right person to pick up the sling. Goliath's mannerisms and actions were specifically designed to taunt and intimidate the Israelites. Just as it was intended, it worked!

> Then he stood and cried out to the armies of Israel, and said to them, "Why have you come out to line up for battle? Am I not a Philistine, and you the servants of Saul? Choose a man for yourselves, and let him come down to me. If he is able to fight with me and kill me, then we will be your servants. But if I prevail against him and kill him, then you shall be our servants and serve us." And the Philistine said, "I defy the armies of Israel this day; give me a man, that we may fight together." When Saul and all Israel heard these words of the Philistine, they were *dismayed and greatly afraid* (1 Samuel 17:8-11, emphasis mine).

The giant cried out. He defied the people of Israel. He defied their leadership and he defied their God. When the people heard his words, they were "dismayed and greatly afraid." It's one thing to be a little apprehensive, but another thing altogether to be greatly afraid. The people were so intimidated by this man that for forty days, not one single person in the entire nation was willing to fight him.

kill the giant.

David refused to be intimidated by Goliath's size or his words. The key to his success is found in his conversation with Saul. He tells Saul that when he compares the battle before him with his past victories over predators attacking his sheep:

> Your servant has killed both lion and bear; and this uncircumcised Philistine will be like one of them, seeing he has defied the armies of the living God" (1 Samuel 17:36).

David understood that the size of his obstacle was not relevant. He knew what God could do. He had seen it demonstrated before. To David it didn't matter if his obstacle was a lion, a bear, or a giant. To David, each was just an obstacle, something that needed to be overcome; size did not matter. Sometimes we overanalyze our obstacle to the point that it appears much stronger than it actually is. Right now, stop focusing on the strength of your obstacle, and take that energy and focus on how to beat it!

Instead of focusing on the strength of our obstacle, we should take that energy and focus on how to beat it!

Always Trust Your Source

The biggest battle David would face was not against a giant, but against his own self-doubt. David could not afford to trust in himself; he had to trust his Source, the One he had depended on for the majority of his life. In order to defeat this physical giant, he first had to overcome the mental giant of his own lack of ability. For David, the battle against Goliath was not an exhibition match in which he could prove his fighting skills. David realized that this victory would not be won through his own strength, but rather from the strength of the Lord. The only reason he had the courage to step out into that valley and challenge the giant was because he had an unshakeable trust in the Lord.

When we trust in ourselves, we will fall miserably short of our goals. However, when we trust in the Lord, there are no limits to what we can accomplish and who we can become. Misguided trust is deceiving and will cause us to second-guess the goals and objectives of our life.

Over the years I've seen people place their trust in areas that are weak and unsustainable. When you place your trust in things that are shallow and temporary, you will always be disappointed and left still searching for answers. Let's contrast Saul and David: Saul's faith was in his army, while David's trust was in the Lord. Saul's kingdom was short-lived; in fact, he only reigned in Israel for about twenty years. David's kingdom lasted about forty years, roughly twice as long. If we take this time span literally and apply it as a principle in our lives, it means we will do twice as much in our life if we will only trust in God! David's trust wasn't created in that specific moment either. His trust was sustained through a lifetime of serving and following God. Take a few moments before continuing to read, and reaffirm your trust in the Lord by praying and expressing your confidence in Him.

Timing Is Everything

The final key to David's defeat of self-doubt was found in his timing. When David walked up on the scene of an intimidated army being challenged on a daily basis by an unhinged giant, he knew he had to act immediately. There was no time to waste; something had to be done—and it had to be done *now*.

In life, timing plays a huge role in many of the things that we do. We wake up, go to work, get off work, go to church, and more, all at specific times. When dealing with people, timing is critical and affects how they will respond greatly. When your boss is displaying signs of fatigue and overall grouchiness, it's probably not the best time to ask off for vacation or that big raise you were hoping for. When a child perceives that his or her parents are in an unusually good mood, it may be just the right time to ask for that "special" Christmas present. In this story, David saw that the timing was critical to his success.

The things you are afraid to confront today, you may be forced to confront tomorrow.

If David had waited and returned home in order to prepare himself, the outcome could have been much different. As he was home training, someone else may have stepped up, been killed by Goliath, and all would have been lost. Israel could have been defeated. David knew he had to act immediately because this giant was not getting any less aggressive. In my last book, *The Left-Handed Warrior*, I titled a chapter, "Pull the Trigger." It was written to encourage people to take a leap of faith when they felt the urging of God to do so. There are seasons in our life when we need to sit still, but there are other ones in which we cannot afford to wait any longer.

Doubt is only as powerful as you choose to allow it to be.

The longer the giants were allowed to stay on the earth, the greater their influence would become. Somebody had to act and extinguish this evil race that threatened to steal the promise from God's people. The things you are afraid to confront today, you may be forced to confront tomorrow. As you wait and procrastinate, the giant of self-doubt never retreats; it only grows larger and more dangerous. When self-doubt begins to be evident in your life, it must be stopped immediately. Don't validate your self-doubt by saying things like, "I can never do this," or "I know I'll never be able to learn that." You can always do more than you think, and you can always go further than you currently realize.

David knew that waiting was not an option. Goliath wasn't leaving, the Israelites were not advancing, and

kill the giant.

God's promise was not being realized. This standoff would find no healthy resolution until somebody decided to step up. History applauds the fact that David decided to do it, and do it now! *So let's do it, and do it now!* Think of three things that you can do right now to help move your plans into action.

From David we learn about these special keys that helped him not only kill a real-life giant, but also overcome the giant of self-doubt within.

As we put these five keys into practice, our weaknesses begin to shrink and we realize that we are capable of much more than we thought we were. When we move beyond our past, effectively handle criticism, refuse to be intimidated, and trust our Source instead of our self, the doubt that plagues our progress is quickly defeated.

The magnitude of your victories remains to be seen; only history will tell how big they will be.

I've seen these keys work in various areas of my own life: from waterskiing, to standing in front of people, to handling personal affairs, and more. Doubt is only as powerful as you choose to allow it to be. My encouragement to you in this chapter is to no longer run from your doubt, but begin to confront it head-on. The giant was staring the Israelites in the face. His taunts, intimidation, and defiance would be there as long as they allowed it. Today, make a choice and confront your giant. Don't be bullied any longer and don't let your own doubt keep you from your victory.

David's victory that day wasn't just a personal victory, it was a national victory. Even he did not realize how great a victory he would experience as he chose to engage the giant. The magnitude of your victories remains to be seen; only history will tell how big they will be. I can't promise that you will always win, but when doubt is left unchecked, you will usually lose. I want to close this chapter with one of my favorite verses from the Bible, let these words resonate within you as you go out and defeat your giant!

> Yet in all these things we are more than conquerors through Him who loved us (Romans 8:37).

Chapter 4: The Dream Is Possible

Have you ever asked a young child the classic question, "What do you want to be when you grow up?" If you have, the answers are usually pretty impressive. Seldom will a child dream of a monotonous, nine-to-five, pencil-pushing, boring, can't-wait-to-get-off-of-work kind of job. When a child speaks on this subject, it comes out as this overflow of young and innocent dreams that are not hampered by the limitations of the word *impossible*.

Sometimes kids dream of being firefighters, police officers, airline pilots, astronauts, doctors, presidents, teachers, and more. Kids usually think big, they dream big, they speak big; it's almost as if their thinking regarding the possibilities in life are limitless. What is it that makes a child's perspective so much different than that of most adults?

Something happens during the span of time between that innocent little dreamer and a responsibility-laden adult. As a child, we are able to imagine everything as possible, but as an adult, our big dreams begin to feel like nothing more than wishful thinking. The older we get, the larger the gap between the word *dream* and the word *achieve.*

When a child sees the future, they see it absent of complications and obstacles. Kids don't often understand financial barriers, lack of opportunity in a certain region, racial bias, or other hindrances to their progress. As adults, we are often programmed to think more about what *can't* happen as opposed to what *can* happen. For some, the constant hindrances to accomplishment finally give way to surrender. Many feel like their dreams are impossible and better off left for others.

As adults, we are often programmed to think more about what can't happen as opposed to what can happen.

The child sees only through the lens of possibility. They see people who have achieved, but don't have the experience of personal failure that might prevent them from taking risks. Sometimes the child dreamer within us chooses to be silent; feelings of failure, impossibility, and lack of opportunity take over. For many, it's easier to dream in silence than it is to actively pursue something we fear will end in disappointment. Some adults sadly live a life in which their dreams are broken, accomplishments are few, and their initiative to dream has been quieted. Does it really have to be that way? Is there a way for us to tap into that little child deep inside of us once again and begin to believe that the dream is still possible?

Chapter 4: The Dream Is Possible

What is it that's so special in a child that they can believe in things like the tooth fairy, Santa Claus, monsters under the bed, and more? The same innocence that allows them to believe in mythical figures, also allows them to dream in such a daring way, a way that becomes off-limits to most adults. Much of the time, kids have a unique advantage over adults. They have not yet been jaded by a society that is largely programmed to focus on obstacles instead of opportunities.

When's the last time you actually enjoyed watching political advertising on television? If you pay attention, you'll notice those ads have more mud-slinging than a South Georgia pigpen. The motivation they try to bring in rallying the troops is focused solely on how terrible their opponent is. Few ads inspire or give hope; most are focused on demeaning the other person and exposing their terrible track record.

Have you ever glanced at the tabloid magazines which are usually strategically placed at the checkout line of your local grocery store? The headlines are not only weird and far-fetched, but often they are very negative. These companies would not continue to churn out this constant dribble of ill-informed garbage unless they were making money. In other words, there is something about negativity that attracts a certain audience—and they are buying it at a steady rate.

If you take the time to sit down and watch the evening news, the majority of the stories center on negative themes. There is always another story about murder,

kill the giant.

burglary, embezzlement and so on. These programs would not hold their ratings unless there was a demand for this type of news. When you really begin to think about it, much of our society seems to thrive on other people's misfortune.

I believe that much of the negativity that constantly swirls around our society has become a giant, its own destructive force that has an adverse impact on our ability to dream. With such a strong, negative message, it sometimes feels like our hopes are difficult to attain at best, and at worst, utterly unachievable. Like the contents of a suitcase that has to be pushed down in order to close, our hope can be compressed by the messaging of our culture. However, that dreamer inside us is still alive—and much like a small child, though all grown up, that dreamer is still ambitious and eager to reach the highest possible goals.

> The all-too-familiar voices
> of doubt and small thinking
> can easily become a giant
> that attempts to reduce our
> dreams to nothing more than a
> passing thought.

The little child within you—the one that doesn't understand the word *impossible*, that doesn't comprehend that obstacles exist—that innocent child within you longs to dream again. What would you dare to attempt if there were no limitations? What if money was not an obstacle?

Chapter 4: The Dream Is Possible

What if you had the right connections to consult or learn from absolutely anyone in the world? What if you had the ability to take all the constraints off your dreams? What would they look like?

The child dreamer has yet to feel the heavy weight of the stifling impact of the negativity of the world. The all-too-familiar voices of doubt and small thinking can easily become a giant that attempts to reduce our dreams to nothing more than a passing thought. Since these thoughts are not able to find the fertile soil of hope and ambition, they disappear and may never surface again. Jesus gave us a unique approach to dealing with what many have named "childlike" faith.

> Then they brought little children to Him, that He might touch them; but the disciples rebuked those who brought them. But when Jesus saw it, He was greatly displeased and said to them, "Let the little children come to Me, and do not forbid them; for of such is the kingdom of God. Assuredly, I say to you, whoever does not receive the kingdom of God as a little child will by no means enter it." And He took them up in His arms, laid His hands on them, and blessed them (Mark 10:13-16).

At this time, Jesus was in the region of Judea, surrounded by a large multitude of people. Jesus taught on the subject of marriage and reminded the people of the intrinsic value of God's plan in holy matrimony. It was during this serious discussion of adult matters that some people began bringing little children to Jesus so

He could touch them. They were looking for the rabbi's blessing, which was a common practice in their culture.

Jesus' disciples most likely felt that the timing of these people was a bit out of order. In response, they rebuked the people and forbid them to bring the children. Jesus could have easily allowed this to happen and remained silent. To correct His disciples publicly would both embarrass them and also require Him to confront His own followers in front of the whole crowd that had gathered. Jesus not only corrected His disciples and the situation, but He used it as a teachable moment.

During this serious, instructional discussion on marriage and divorce, Jesus stopped everything and visibly showed His displeasure with the attitude of His disciples. Instead of pushing the kids away and encouraging them to come back at a more appropriate time, He interrupted Himself so the parents would bring the children closer. Jesus was clearly making a point, but was He driving at something even deeper?

The key is found in His response in verse 15:

> "Assuredly, I say to you, whoever does not receive the kingdom of God as a little child will by no means enter it."

What does it mean, to "receive" the kingdom of God as a child? I believe it goes back to that little child dreamer, you know, the one who's inside you and ready to dream and believe big. A child believes without doubting and questioning; a child simply takes one's word and accepts what is being said.

Jesus was answering questions from the crowd. Some of them were trying to back Him into a corner to find some sort of fault with Him. There were religious people there, many who were trying to catch Jesus in a violation or contradiction of the Law. Just as this atmosphere of doubt and negativity swirled around Him, the children just wanted to be touched by the Master. The kids had a unique ability to cut beyond the unbelief, and focus on the only thing that was truly important: Jesus.

Jesus was focusing in a positive way on the same thing that the disciples were focusing on negatively. What the disciples saw as a lack of judgment and poor timing, Jesus saw as unhindered, bold, and opportunistic faith. In the disciples' minds, the kids were interrupting and distracting Jesus from things that were more important. In Jesus' mind, as evidenced by what He said, the innocence of the children and the extension of their faith was giving them access to the kingdom. In fact, Jesus even said that the kingdom must be entered by those who were like children.

The children weren't distracted by the crowds of people and the protocol of a religious society. They were simply focused on their desire at that specific time. There may well have been others in the crowd that day who had needs, but felt they should wait until a "better" time. Maybe they missed their opportunity. Perhaps they talked themselves out of an opportunity to have an

kill the giant.

audience with Jesus. What if their miracle was just on the other side of a simple question? They, as well as we, will never know.

While many may have been consumed with the proper order and possible thoughts of rejection, the kids were focused on Jesus and got exactly what they came for. The crowds were concerned with the thoughts of the other people, while the children were concerned with their purpose.

Don't Let Fear Hold You Back

Your dreams are too important to be defined by your fear. While you are steeped in mediocrity, there are people who are racing ahead and refusing to listen to all the reasons why they can't achieve what they set out to do. If you don't allow the crowd or your own failure to dampen your spirit, the child within you will rise to the occasion.

Your dreams are too important to
be defined by your fear.

I remember when I was learning to ride a bike. My dad held the back of the bicycle seat and paced himself with me as I pedaled along. When he felt like I was getting a good feel for the balance, he let go for short durations of time. As he did, I began to sway back and forth without the guidance of his strong hand on the seat. He reacted by simply grabbing the seat again until I regained a steady balance.

Chapter 4: The Dream Is Possible

As time went on, the span of time between turning me loose and holding onto the seat increased. Eventually, his hand was on the seat just to make me think he was guiding me, when in truth I was doing the balancing myself. I remember the day when I began to pedal downhill and was moving so quickly that he was having a hard time keeping up. Unbeknownst to me, he completely let go! After going a pretty good distance, I realized he was no longer holding on. I turned back to confirm my fears, began to sway, and lost my balance. This ended up in a violent crash at the bottom of the hill (at least in my childlike mind it was violent).

Truthfully, it was a simple tumble and all was well. I had no real injuries, but what I did have was very valuable. When I looked back up the hill and saw how far I had gone on my own, I realized I could maintain my balance without additional help. I could ride a bike all by myself! What looked like a failure with a toppled bike lying on top of me was actually a perspective change that said, "I can do this." With that, I jumped back on the bike and took off riding like I had been riding for years.

Sometimes the bumps and bruises of failure discourage us when they should be motivating us. The big things in life are never simple; sometimes our greatest accomplishments will come after our greatest failures. What if I had never gotten back up on that bike again? What if I had been so upset about my crash that I chose to never ride again? I would be a grown man who

kill the giant.

never learned how to ride a bike. Failure can be a great motivator if we learn to be more like a child.

Sometimes our greatest
accomplishments will come after
our greatest failures.

Children will typically gravitate toward the good in things and seldom see the bad until it is pointed out. For example, nobody has ever been born with a racist attitude. Racism isn't natural; it is a learned behavior. And a child's mindset isn't small, but it can gradually become that way as a result of personal experience and the influence of others. I have to believe that when Jesus drew attention to the children, he was speaking about a whole lot more than just simple innocence.

Perspective

As I write these words, my family and I are vacationing in the mountains of northern Georgia. We try to come to this area at least once every couple of years. We enjoy the crisp mountain air, the good country cooking, the beautiful wildlife, and the natural scenery. Something about staying deep in the woods always brings a greater reverence for God's creative power.

To get to our little place in the woods requires a long ride up the mountain. The twists and turns of a skinny mountain road can be a bit unnerving but offer breathtaking scenery. The vehicle gets filthy as we splash through the mud, go over bumps, and hang onto narrow corners. The reason we go is to intentionally get away from the crowds and the busyness of everyday life.

The cabin we are staying in has a beautiful view over the Blue Ridge Mountains, and we can see a distance of many miles. Looking over those mountains is an inspiring reminder that the possibilities in life are limitless when you lift up your eyes toward the horizon. When you see the beauty of such an endless landscape, you tend to briefly forget about all the problems and issues you may be facing back home.

One of the things we like to do is hike in the woods right behind our cabin. There's no hiking trail; it's just a good old-fashioned trek through the woods. As we travel down the mountain, we have to be careful of our footing or we will slip and slide. As we travel back up, we also have to be careful, as we can feel the strain on our legs and joints as we push ourselves up the steep incline. My boys and I go on these walks together, but I can't seem to shake the feeling that I'm slowing them down a bit. For some reason, they repeatedly ask the same question over and over, "Dad, are you okay?" Like some others reading these words, we are not as young as we used to be!

On a different note, another thing I've noticed when we walk down the mountain is that the view changes drastically. As we descend, we can no longer see for endless miles; in fact, there are times when we can only see a few yards in front of us. The thick trees and underbrush create a visual blanket that is nearly impossible to pierce. Gone is the view of the endless treetops and the babbling brooks emptying into the nearby river. We are still in the same area. In fact, we are only a short distance from the cabin, but with less elevation, our vantage point has changed dramatically. What happened to the incredible scenery and the beautiful view? The truth is that nothing about the landscape has changed at all; our perspective is different.

Childlike faith is not limited to the qualities of innocence and inexperience, but it is also a special perspective that refuses to think small. To increase our faith, we need to change our perspective. Instead of being overwhelmed by our failures and disappointments, we must use them as tools to help us avoid future pitfalls and mistakes. Remember, the others in the crowd that day had no interaction with Jesus because they did not approach Him with their needs. The children came to Him even when they were viewed as disorderly by the disciples, and their faith was rewarded by Jesus. While others were focused on logistics and protocol, the kids focused only on the possibilities before them.

Sometimes the key to improving our outlook is to purposely see it from a different viewpoint. As adults, we can easily become overwhelmed with the complexities of life. A child, however, has a different perspective. I've never seen a young child visibly shaken because of an unpaid bill, marital problems, or the balance in their retirement account. However, adults are often concerned about these things. When Jesus spoke about the little children, could He have also been referring to the child's perspective on life itself?

Our perspective can steal our ability to dream. Sometimes we have to be able to see past our own problems and give ourselves permission to dream again. The child is an unhindered dreamer—a dreamer with no restraints or barriers, just wide-open opportunities with an unbridled hope for the future. We have to harness the perspective of the child within us and then release that child to believe for things that are bigger than we are.

To increase our faith, we need to change our perspective.

Another characteristic of a child is that they are completely unafraid to think big. When I say big, I mean really big. As mentioned before, when a child speaks of their future, they challenge us when we hear their incredibly ambitious replies. They have not been preconditioned to see obstacles, so they think with huge end results. What would happen if we thought like that? Obviously, children don't have the responsibilities of an adult or the pressures of working. They also don't have the same level of maturity offered through life experiences that adults have, but what if we could find a healthy balance for ourselves? Could we develop a mindset that understands responsibility, remains mature, but still has the capacity to dream big like a child?

kill the giant.

Aim Higher

Sometimes we allow ourselves to settle for thoughts and beliefs that do not stretch us into new territories. It is easier to stay where we are than it is to venture out into the unknown. Children do not think this way at all. Just listen to a child speak; they don't relate to obstacles and boundaries. They haven't been exposed to the world of "I can't" long enough to hold back and restrict their aspirations. A child seldom aims low. Instead, they usually think on a level that aims high, sometimes over-the-top high. We could learn a lot from children and the way they think. It is this very mindset that Jesus speaks of in the famous Sermon on the Mount. As Jesus discussed many important topics ranging from attitude to money, He then focused on the subject of faith.

> "Ask, and it will be given to you; seek, and you will find; knock, and it will be opened to you. For everyone who asks receives, and he who seeks finds, and to him who knocks it will be opened. Or what man is there among you who, if his son asks for bread, will give him a stone? Or if he asks for a fish, will he give him a serpent? If you then, being evil, know how to give good gifts to your children, how much more will your Father who is in heaven give good things to those who ask Him!" (Matthew 7:7-11).

Perhaps Jesus was drawing a parallel between asking and believing for big things and the faith of a child. Notice He put this into context by reflecting on a child asking a parent for specific things. Sometimes people feel like it's somehow out of order or too presumptuous to ask God for very specific things. We are easily made to feel guilty about expectation, and think that we should just do our best to be good because "whatever happens is God's will." However, this thinking is completely opposite to what Jesus' ministry teaches.

The stories of Jesus' life are full of examples in which people came to Him asking for something very specific. People with physical ailments like blinded eyes, deaf ears, and children tormented by seizures, and more, were all brought to Jesus. Those requests were specific. Part of our ability to dream and believe big is to realize that we need supernatural help in order to experience truly supernatural results.

Power of the Tongue

In some part, faith is cultivated in our lives through our ability to verbalize what we believe. Have you ever been thinking about something and surprise yourself by accidentally telling someone else about it? Remember how you felt after that? You may have experienced a sense of holding yourself accountable to that person based on what you said. That thought may have never had much traction, but the moment you said it out loud, it gave birth to action.

A number of years ago, my wife and I had been talking with each other and praying about starting a church. This was something we felt God was placing in our hearts, but there was also a level of apprehension and uncertainty as to what our future would look like, should we choose to move forward. In my first book, I shared in detail about how some of that played out. While talking only with each other, there was safety inside the cocoon of our dream. But the moment we began to share it with others, the climate quickly changed.

Sometimes the lack of verbalizing our dream is the only thing that's keeping us from the support of our dream.

The more we talked about it, the more we realized that this was a call from the Lord. We began by only sharing with our immediate family, and then that circle began to slowly expand as we included our pastor and key accountability partners. What we discovered is that once the proverbial cat was out of the bag, the atmosphere of our faith grew more intense. People began to confirm the call on our lives and the belief in our ability to achieve it.

Once released, the dream inside of our hearts had the opportunity to resonate in the hearts of others. Anyone that's ever been involved in starting a church knows that one of the main hurdles to success is finances. As the atmosphere of faith began to grow, so did the tug on the hearts of other people to help us fund that dream. It was only after we began to verbalize the dream that people began to support it.

Chapter 4: The Dream Is Possible

Often, it's the fear of making ourselves vulnerable to the criticisms or short-sightedness of others that prevents us from verbalizing our dream. Sometimes the lack of verbalizing our dream is the only thing that's keeping us from the support of our dream. Had we been too afraid to share our dream with anyone, it would never have gotten off of the ground. The more we shared with others, the more momentum the dream began to gain.

If you are being stirred right now, I would strongly encourage you to begin speaking what's in your heart to do. You don't have to start by telling everyone; in fact, you can even start by sharing the dream with yourself. As crazy as it may sound, sometimes when you hear yourself speak aloud, it can change the dynamic of your faith. Scripture teaches us this very principle:

> So then faith comes by hearing, and hearing by the word of God (Romans 10:17).

Many take this verse to simply mean that faith is generated when we read the Bible. However, we read that faith comes from *hearing the word of God*. Hearing God's word is not just limited to Bible reading, but can come from many sources. You can hear other people share a confirmation of something that God is speaking to you. God can begin to stir you with His word as you watch or hear a person giving a sermon. We can begin to speak the word that God has planted in our heart out loud and our faith can be strengthened.

kill the giant.

A Lesson from Nature

In order for a dream to begin to develop, it has to be birthed and then released. If you watch the process of a bird laying eggs and then nurturing its young, there are some interesting parallels to the dreams God has given us. The mother bird incubates and protects the eggs until they reach maturity and are ready to hatch. In the same way, a dream has to be protected by praying and being careful not to focus on negativity and doubt. There are many circumstances (and even people) that prove to be nothing more than dream killers. So even as I am encouraging you to share your dream, you also need to be careful with whom you share it. Others' jealousy and envy could threaten your dream and cause you to lose your much-needed focus.

There are many circumstances (and even people) that prove to be nothing more than dream killers

---

After the eggs hatch, the mother bird searches and brings back food for the babies to eat. After much care and some growth, there comes a time when the babies will need to function on their own. Many species of birds actually nudge or even push the babies out of the nest. This is the only way they will learn to fly on their own. The mother cares for them, but if she remains their caregiver for too long it becomes unhealthy and dysfunctional.

Chapter 4: The Dream Is Possible

A dream that is never released becomes dysfunctional. This unfulfilled dream can turn into anger, resentment, and even regret. Part of dream development is to push it out of the comfort of the nest and begin to speak about it to yourself and then with trusted people. The vulnerability phase of speaking the dream is the first step to building the foundation of faith to see that dream fulfill its destiny.

A dream that is never released
becomes dysfunctional.

Dream that Dream!

I began this chapter by referencing how little kids are completely unhindered in their ability to dream. My hope and prayer is that by reading this, you too will begin to dream like a child. Not the immature dream of an idealistic toddler, but an audacious dream given by a God who loves and believes in you. Allow these words to resonate within you, not for the sake of emotional stirring, but for the purpose of accomplishment. There are giants out there that are positioned for defeat, while the world is waiting for a child-dreamer—a dreamer like you—to fulfill your destiny and slay that giant. Don't settle for impossible; immerse yourself in the knowledge that the dream is absolutely possible!

kill the giant.

4: The Dream Is Possible
Action Points

Face Your Obstacles: Begin to awaken the child within you who simply trusts God, no questions asked. Begin praying and asking God to help you find your faith and your dream once again. Make a choice to see obstacles as opportunities to blaze a new trail, as opposed to accepting every closed door as final. Remember, any great thing that has ever been accomplished had to first overcome its share of obstacles.

Refuse to Surrender to Negativity: Begin to quickly identify and dispel negativity when it attempts to leech onto you. This could be that "downer" of a coworker, or even a family member or leader; regardless, start speaking up against their negativity or remove yourself as quickly as possible. Know that the giant of negativity will come your way: It's not a possibility; it is a certainty. One of the key factors to your success will always be how you handle this difficult reality. Of all the presidents we have had in American history, John F. Kennedy held the highest average approval rating during his presidency. Gallup polls showed his average approval rating for his time in office to be 70.1%.[3] That sounds pretty good, but remember this means that roughly 30% of the entire

3. Andrew Dugan and Frank Newport. "Americans Rate JFK as Top Modern President." *Gallup.com*, Gallup, 26 Nov. 2019, https://news.gallup.com/poll/165902/americans-rate-jfk-top-modern-president.aspx.

country *disapproved!* You will probably never get everybody to believe in your dream; you may only get a few or even one, even if that one is you. Negativity has to be destroyed in order for the dream to have a place to grow.

Attack Fear: Begin to positively affirm yourself in the face of fear. Say things like: "I can do this," "I am a smart person," "I have done this successfully before," and "I am destined to succeed." Remember, God is not the creator of fear. Also, remember that God is for you and believes in you. It would be unnatural to scale the world's highest mountain and have absolutely no reservations about it. If you expect to accomplish big things, fear cannot have the final word. Everyone in history who's ever fought a giant had some concerns. As valid as those concerns may have been, they had to be overcome before they would see success. As you pray, aim higher and put your trust in the Lord.

Be Specific: A dream that is unclear is only a thought. Keep internalizing your dream and talking it through until it becomes crystal clear. There is a reason why the leading industries in our world focus on specific sectors and sometimes individual products. Most businesses don't repair lawnmowers and run a steak house at the same time. Their vision is clear, their dream is specific, and their end result can be measured because there are parameters of clarity around the dream. When you begin to act in faith and pray for God to give you favor and help you accomplish your dream, be specific. Pray for obstacles to be removed, specific goals and deadlines to be met, and believe Him to do what only He can do.

Speak the Dream: Hearing yourself vocalize your dream gives it life! If you never declare what your dream is, the dream will eventually die with you. Be selective regarding who you choose to confide in, especially in the beginning, but sharing your dream will add value and draw resources. Speaking your dream will also help you further clarify exactly what has been put in your heart to accomplish.

Chapter 5: Tenacious

Like many middle-aged men, I continued a number of poor eating habits from my teenage years that were never resolved. In fact, I would have to say those habits probably got worse as I grew older. I have always looked forward to sitting down each night right before bed and eating a massive bowl of sugary cereal, or better yet; a heaping bowl of ice cream scooped over a hot piece of cake. As a teenager and young adult, I had been very athletic, playing football, racquetball, and other sports. However, as time progressed, my level of physical activity slowed down. These habits eventually caught up with me when I noticed I was packing on several pounds each year.

I realized it was time for me to do something about it, so several years ago I began the dreaded "D" word: a diet. As I began, I was immediately forced to see how bad my eating habits actually were. I was drinking a number of sodas each day in addition to quite a few other bad eating choices. I noticed that my new way of eating would not allow these behaviors to continue, not if I planned on any level of success. During the first week or so, I suffered from sugar withdrawal. This struggle became real. I felt bad, my energy was dragging, and my wife would probably tell you I was a little moody (okay,

kill the giant.

I admit I was very moody). I didn't know if I would be able to continue another week, much less as a permanent lifestyle change.

The hardest part for me was going to bed without my sugary snack. The truth is, I wasn't really hungry; it had just become a habit—a really bad habit. As you probably know, habits are difficult to develop and even harder to break. However, with the encouragement of my wife and kids and the truth-telling full length mirror in my bedroom, I decided to stick it out for at least a two-week period. As I progressed closer to that time frame, I realized that I was feeling a bit better. I was slightly less irritable, and I also felt like I had a little more energy.

I remember stepping on the scale for the first time since I began the diet. I had made a commitment to not weigh myself until after the two weeks was up. As I looked down at the numbers, I could hardly believe what I saw. In those two weeks of pretty serious change, I had lost eight pounds! I told my wife about my new discovery and she commented that she could tell I was making some progress. That was the encouragement I was looking for and the motivation I needed!

I'm pretty sure that if I had weighed myself and hadn't lost any weight, I would have made a beeline straight to the store for some cake, and then topped it off with a pile of ice cream. However, since I had made so much progress and suffered through two weeks of torture, I valued the reward over the pain. This not only helped me to stay consistent with the diet, but now I was ready to kick it up a notch.

I continued eating very strictly; and over the next several months, I was able to lose thirty-five pounds. I am happy to report that it's now been several years and I have been able to keep the weight off. How did I manage this? This wasn't some secret formula or some expensive diet program; it was just by making healthy choices. However, the real key for me was the momentum created by the success I had which motivated me to work harder.

Don't Give Up!

At any given time during my weight loss, it would have been very easy to fall off the proverbial wagon. As we compare pain to reward, sometimes the pain is significant enough that our judgment is clouded and convinces us to give up or give in. We've all worked for specific goals: saving money, training for an athletic event, advancing our education, and the list goes on. All of these can be very difficult, but the payoff at completion is usually well worth the cost.

As we fight against the giants threatening our success, we can become tired. As discussed in Chapter One, giants don't die easily, and giving up is sometimes the easiest thing to do. The giant of self-doubt or the insecurity that keeps you from taking risks is very real and won't give up without a fight. Sometimes that fight is a long one.

One of the great employees we have in our organization is part of our trusted maintenance crew.

kill the giant.

He's a hard worker with a real dedication to details and timely task completion. Whenever there's a particularly important job that requires being done correctly, this man is the one to call. He has been with us for many years, and has proven himself over and over to be trustworthy and dependable.

As a military veteran, he developed a bit of a drinking problem in the service, which continued in his life long after his career ended. He has shared how this caused him and his family a great deal of pain over the years. Alcohol is a true robber. I've seen it destroy marriages, finances, health, and more. What I love about this guy, though, is the fact that he has robbed the robber!

His testimony is powerful. He grew up without a strong family cohesiveness that many take for granted. His drinking was a habit, but it was also a bandage to temporarily cover the pain of his troubled past. When he met Jesus, his life was changed as he went full force into serving the Lord and the church. He was also able to quit drinking almost cold turkey, although he has had a few slip-ups along the way.

Defeating your problems requires
daily self-encouragement and a
focus on the reward.

Many would look at him and say "Congratulations, you have beaten your giant!" This is true. It would also be true, however, to note that even though he has been successful in not drinking for many years, *the temptation*

114

to turn back still exists. He will tell you that winning over alcohol is a daily battle. There is never a day when he doesn't think about having a single drink, or worse yet, going completely off the deep end and falling prey to the bondage of alcohol once again.

When facing the daily struggles of the issues that you are up against, it is important to understand that *the battle is ongoing*. People who have lost weight and kept it off, understand they can never go back to their old eating habits. Yes, they have overcome their struggle, but they can never become overly confident and fall back into the same trap again. People who have overcome insecurities will tell you that those nagging voices still exist in their head; they've just learned how to manage them and live beyond their noise.

You will not fully dedicate
yourself to things in which you
place no value.

Defeating your nemesis, or your nemeses, is not a switch that can be thrown in which the problem simply vanishes from existence. Defeating your problems requires daily self-encouragement and a focus on the reward. For the maintenance worker who was mentioned earlier, the reward of success far outweighed the pain of quitting. Quitting alcohol meant a drastically improved home life, a more stable career opportunity, and a much better outlook in terms of his physical health.

kill the giant.

One of the ways to overcome your obstacles is to take the time to really think about the advantages of success. You will not fully dedicate yourself to things in which you place no value. When you truly consider the reward tied to success, it will raise that worth to such a place that you will be more willing to invest in the outcome. Only a tenacious attitude will see you past the setbacks, discouragement, and the uphill battle before you, allowing you to overcome in the areas you struggle in once and for all.

A Biblical Example

In the classic story of David and Goliath there is an often overlooked, little detail that preceded that battle. This detail is very significant as it played a vital part in David's decision to face the giant. As you may recall, David was simply delivering some food to his brothers who were part of Israel's army. He was not part of the military; in fact, he had never even fought against another human being before. As he approached the battle scene, he quickly recognized that something was a little off—well, very off. The people of Israel weren't advancing in battle; instead, they were cowering in fear while a giant named Goliath belted out threats against them.

As David approached he began to ask people what was going on. He soon realized this was a bad situation. Scripture records what happened as the people responded to the giant:

Chapter 5: Tenacious

> And all the men of Israel, when they saw the man,
> fled from him and were dreadfully afraid. So the
> men of Israel said, "Have you seen this man who has
> come up? Surely he has come up to defy Israel; and
> it shall be that the man who kills him the king will
> enrich with great riches, will give him his daughter,
> and give his father's house exemption from taxes in
> Israel" (1 Samuel 17:24-25).

As David begins talking with the men, they tell him
about the reward involved for killing the giant. It's a
pretty hefty one too. The victorious warrior would be
given money, granted the king's daughter as wife, and
that warrior's household would be exempt from taxes
forever. That's what I call a reward! As David heard this
list, he asked for clarification:

> Then David spoke to the men who stood by him,
> saying, "What shall be done for the man who kills
> this Philistine and takes away the reproach from
> Israel? For who is this uncircumcised Philistine,
> that he should defy the armies of the living God?"
> And the people answered him in this manner,
> saying, "So shall it be done for the man who kills
> him" (1 Samuel 17:26-27).

David got a full breakdown of the reward, but just
to make sure he heard correctly, he asked someone else
to tell him again. Obviously, David was doing some
serious contemplation and considering whether or not
the reward was worth the risk. As a final measure (and

to be absolutely certain he had heard correctly) David inquires yet again.

> And David said, "What have I done now? Is there not a cause?" Then he turned from him toward another and said the same thing; and these people answered him as the first ones did (1 Samuel 17:29-30).

Assess the Reward

Yes, you heard that correctly. David had been told the specifics of the reward three different times. There is a part of overcoming our obstacles that is spiritual. This means that God fights on our behalf and defeats what we cannot defeat. The outcome of the battle between David and Goliath was a result of God's intervention. However, make no mistake about this: David's tenacity positioned him as the man God used.

There can be many motivators
in life, but they usually boil
down to one of two things; pain
and reward.

David's tenacity was formed by realizing that Goliath was an insult and a scourge upon godly Israel. He knew that the people of Israel were favored and that God would fight for them, but David was also motivated by the hope of personal gain. David got the details of the reward three times from three different sources. He

Chapter 5: Tenacious

asked these questions because he wanted to see if it was worth it to risk his life to fight this giant. I want you to understand this truth: Had there been no reward, we wouldn't have the story of David and Goliath.

God won the victory, but the tenacity of David positioned him to be that vessel. Why did David ask repeatedly about the reward? As David was weighing risk versus reward, he wanted to hear over and over what the reward would actually be. As his focus began to dial in on the "why" of the battle, David could clearly see the value. David would not have been motivated to risk his life for a simple pat on the back, but this reward made it worthwhile.

There can be many motivators in life, but they usually boil down to one of two things; pain and reward. Things that are hurting you can give you the push necessary to make changes to stop the pain. Also, if you see a significant reward at the finish line, this can serve as a great motivator too. Kids are sometimes motivated to do their chores with the reward of an allowance, while they can also be motivated by the threat of punishment. In the story of David and Goliath, both principles are at work. The pain was the ongoing threat of the giant and the implication of allowing him to exist. The reward was a huge payout being offered by the king. David had to consider both of these motivators before making his decision to step onto the battlefield that day.

kill the giant.

Why Are You Fighting?

To win against the obstacles you face, you have to be able to clearly define the reward and constantly remind yourself of what that is. If you see no real reward and you are only acting on an emotional whim, you will most likely give up long before you succeed. I have learned that there are many more starters than there are finishers. Anyone can start a marathon, but few have the endurance to see it all the way to completion. Remember, the obstacles you face will not be beaten with a quick-sprint mindset, they will be beaten through a long-term commitment if you want to see complete success.

Clearly define the reward and
constantly remind yourself of
what that is.

As we read the story of David, we cannot help but be impressed by his bravery and his faith. His willingness to fight a man who nobody else would face is a remarkable undertaking. The fact that he actually won puts the story over the top. This is certainly one of those Hall of Fame stories. Another fact about David though, is that Goliath was the first giant he killed, but it wouldn't be his last. As mentioned before, the world is made up of two types of people: starters and finishers. David wasn't just a starter. David was a finisher in the truest sense of the word.

Chapter 5: Tenacious

The Line Destroyed

In Chapter One, I told you that the giants were eventually extinguished from the earth. This wasn't because they died of natural causes; it was because someone sought them out and killed them one by one. The person who would be successful at this task could be no mere "starter"; this would require a "finisher," someone who was unapologetically tenacious.

The same attitude and faith that caused David to overcome Goliath would also drive him to successfully wipe out all the known strongholds occupied by giants. David knew that if the giants remained, there would always be a threat lurking in the shadows. As a shepherd, and later as a king, he knew he could never be safe as long as another giant existed.

Sometimes we are fooled by thinking that obstacles in our lives which aren't posing problems right now are better left alone. Remember the weeds in the first chapter? If they are not completely uprooted, those little issues will eventually become big issues. We must deal with them in a timely manner.

Before David was the king of Israel, there was another king by the name of Saul. Saul was in leadership during the battle in which Goliath was killed. He was there when his army was afraid to fight the giant. Saul didn't have the courage to fight the giant himself or to even send out a representative who would fight on behalf of the nation. This inability to face the giant was not a one-time event in Saul's life; he was like this throughout his entire reign as king. Saul never killed any of the giants that plagued the land. Saul's mindset was, "If you don't bother them, they won't bother you." This may sound like a good policy, but it proved false.

As Saul continued to build his kingdom, training his army, and negotiating with the countries around him, the giants continued to thrive. Much like the obstacles in our own lives, it's easier not to stir things up than to dig deep and dedicate ourselves to long-term success. The lie that Saul bought into was that if the giants weren't bothering him, then the giants weren't any bother.

> The lie that Saul bought into was that if the giants weren't bothering him, then the giants weren't any bother.

The obstacles of self-doubt, insecurity, a poverty mindset, a lack of faith, a fear of failure, addictions, and more will never go away on their own. These obstacles not only remain intact within us, but when left alone, they grow and become stronger and more dangerous. Just because an issue is not staring you in the face right this minute does not mean that it is harmless or nonexistent. David had the foresight to see what Saul could not see. Saul was self-absorbed in his own notoriety and too shallow to see the Big Picture. Never be satisfied with only a small victory. Know that God has much more in store for you than an occasional win. He has destined you to live as a continual winner.

Chapter 5: Tenacious

Yet in all these things we are more than conquerors
through Him who loved us (Romans 8:37).

What Saul was unable or unwilling to do, David was
driven to do. Saul may have made excuses as to why he
didn't want to mess with the giants of the land: It was too
messy, too risky, too scary, or just impossible. Whatever
his excuses may have been, David did not think that way.
Never make excuses for what you lack the tenacity to do.
Excuses have never accomplished anything. If you're
reading these words and feel a little uneasy, there's
probably good reason. Don't feel too bad; we've all been
guilty of making excuses for what we don't want to do.

```
          Never make excuses for what you
                lack the tenacity to do.
```

Everyone has an excuse as to why they haven't saved
more money. Most people can tell you why they haven't
chosen a life of physical fitness. Many will be able to
explain why they aren't any closer to God than they
are. People will tell you why they weren't good parents,
good employees, good spouses—and list could go on for
another book or two. Let me bottom line it for you: We
make excuses for anything for which we've become too
comfortable with to correct.

While Saul was making excuses, David was killing
giants! Some people are always talking about what they
want to do, while other people are doing what they want
to do. Saul goes down in history as the guy with few

military wins and no major victories. He made excuses for his lack of obedience, his sin, and his failure. Saul was unsuccessful because he was anything but tenacious.

David didn't stop at killing only one giant on the battlefield as a young shepherd boy. David became known as a powerful warrior and a mighty man of faith who had many victories. David's first giant was Goliath, but this wouldn't be his last. Here is a telling chronicle of David's life and leadership as king of Israel:

> Now it happened afterward that war broke out at Gezer with the Philistines, at which time Sibbechai the Hushathite killed Sippai, who was one of the sons of the giant. And they were subdued. Again there was war with the Philistines, and Elhanan the son of Jair killed Lahmi the brother of Goliath the Gittite, the shaft of whose spear was like a weaver's beam. Yet again there was war at Gath, where there was a man of great stature, with twenty-four fingers and toes, six on each hand and six on each foot; and he also was born to the giant. So when he defied Israel, Jonathan the son of Shimea, David's brother, killed him. These were born to the giant in Gath, and they fell by the hand of David and by the hand of his servants (1 Chronicles 20:4-8).

While Saul was making excuses,
David was killing giants!

Chapter 5: Tenacious

David, unlike Saul, didn't just sit back and pretend the giants didn't exist. He and his men sought them out and purposely endeavored to eradicate them from the earth. David was unwilling to allow these men to live during his reign with no resistance. He knew that if they existed, they would eventually cause problems for his people in the future. Like the obstacles in our lives, the giants have to be hunted down and destroyed or they will show themselves, and usually at the most inopportune times.

These verses also show us another important truth. After this era of history, the Bible is completely silent about the existence of giants. There are no more references to giants after the reign of David because David was the king who was willing to do what his predecessor was unwilling to do. David didn't just slay one giant: *He slayed all the remaining giants on the earth!* All the judges and military leaders before David never accomplished what he did. The first king of Israel could not do what David did. David's accomplishment wasn't easy, but it was a matter of necessity.

Like the obstacles in our lives,
the giants have to be hunted
down and destroyed or they will
show themselves, and usually at
the most inopportune times.

You have to understand that David was not just some great leader genetically predisposed to giant-killing. He was simply a man of faith with an attitude that wouldn't

kill the giant.

let him quit until the job was done. In other words, the character traits that David had can also be ours. David had his weaknesses too. We have read of his infamous act of adultery. David was not the favorite child in his household, as evidenced by the disdain of his brothers. However, with all of these things against him, David was the one man in history who did what no other man had ever done. David rid the earth of the evil giants, every last one of them.

A Lifetime of Commitment

David's success wasn't accomplished in a two-week stint of emotional momentum in which he felt like he could conquer the world. Neither did he defeat all the giants in one single battle. The adrenaline rush of fighting with a thousand men did not transform David into some kind of superhero. The fight between David and Goliath took place when David was only a youth. In fact, his youth was one of Saul's reasons for not allowing David to fight Goliath at first. The scripture in Chronicles that was just cited took place much later in David's life, after he had been king for many years. David's experience of seeking out and killing giants consumed a large part of his life and reign as king of Israel. His success wasn't overnight. It was the product of a lifetime of dedication.

Don't allow your temporary losses to rob you of your permanent victory.

Chapter 5: Tenacious

Defeating our obstacles must be a lifetime commitment. This doesn't mean we won't see results in the beginning, but it does mean we have to be in it for the long haul.

> Yesterday is gone. Tomorrow has not yet come.
> We have only today. Let us begin.
> —Mother Teresa[4]

This statement is an example of a commitment that was not short-lived. Mother Teresa was a voice for those who had no voice for the majority of her life. We don't remember her legacy through one defining moment; we remember her legacy in a lifetime of dedication to a cause she believed in. In fact, she believed in her cause so strongly that she brought us along to believe in it as well. This didn't happen in a day, a year, or even a decade; this happened over a lifetime.

Don't allow your temporary losses to rob you of your permanent victory. Everyone—and I mean everyone— will suffer defeat many times in their lives. Winning is not determined by how often you get knocked down, but by how often you get back up, dust yourself off, and go at it again. A tenacious attitude is important for lifelong success, but that attitude is never instantaneous. The bumps and bruises of life are powerful reminders of our fragility, but they cannot defeat you unless you surrender.

---

4. Goalcasthttp. "Top 20 Most Inspiring Mother Teresa Quotes." *Goalcast*, 19 Aug. 2019, https://www.goalcast.com/2017/04/10/top-20-most-inspiring-mother-teresa-quotes/.

kill the giant.

The tenacious refuse to surrender, refuse to quit, refuse to lose, and will never give up on their dream.

You may not be naturally tenacious. Truth be told, maybe you feel more like a lamb than a lion. Tenacity is developed over time. It is not a personality trait, but a mindset. You can be as gentle as a lamb, yet determined and strong as any lion. Your tenacity can be strengthened and your resolve galvanized as you continue to grow and pursue your goals. Never feel like you don't have what it takes to be tenacious. You may have been a quitter or weak in the past, but you can begin to steer that ship in the right direction today. It's never too late to start being who you've always wanted to be! The key is to start. When you fail, start again; and if you keep failing, keep starting. You might wonder, "How many times am I supposed to keep starting over?" My answer would be, "As many times as it takes."

> It's never too late to start being who you've always wanted to be!

This chapter started with the story of my own weight loss and lifestyle change. For me, this was much more than just losing a few pounds and getting healthier. This was about proving to myself that I could accomplish something that I was fearful of trying to do. The weight loss wasn't fast and it certainly wasn't easy, but the results were worth the pain of change.

I have always been on a constant quest of self-improvement, so this concept has helped me in other areas too. I want to be a better husband, father, pastor, and friend, but I know that if I am going to be successful in these areas, I have to change. Change, growth, and development have one thing in common: a degree of pain is required. Never allow the evasion of pain to rob you of the reward you would gain through success. The person you want to be will emerge from the person you already are.

In a moment of hunger you may question the diet you chose, but don't give up and lose your reward. As you continue to be consistent, faithful, and diligent, you can make great strides to see your goals accomplished. Never allow the pain to steal your victory. Be confident that you can and will succeed in time.

The person you want to be will
emerge from the person you
already are.

In the next chapter, we will discuss some of the setbacks you may face. It is important to keep focused, even when things go awry. Never forget this: Tenacity is worth its weight in gold. Your tenacity will become more valuable than your skills, experience, and training. Keep pushing, keep believing, and never give up! One common theme among great achievers is their strong sense of urgency for what they believe in. You will only live and die for those things for which you truly have a passion and believe in wholeheartedly.

5: Tenacious
Action Points

Refuse to Give Up: Have you quit something or more than one thing? Make a list of them and decide right now that you are going to pick them back up and try again. It could be something as simple as a hobby, a weight-loss plan, or maybe even something more difficult like finishing a degree. It is a powerful exercise to show yourself you still have what it takes to succeed, even if it has been many years since you've tried. Nothing great will be easy, and few things that are easy will be great. Develop a mindset that says: I will not quit, regardless of what happens. There are countless examples of athletes, politicians, and millionaires who could have easily quit along the way. Many were told they could not do something, but they did it anyway. Staying on track doesn't guarantee success, but quitting guarantees failure!

Nothing great will be easy, and few things that are easy will be great.

Define Your Goals: What are your long-term goals? Write them down and put them up somewhere where you see them on the daily basis. Physical, financial, professional, whatever they are: put them in writing! You can't value something of which you are unsure. If you are negotiating the price of a car, you would need to do some research to determine its value first. If you don't even know the value, how would you know a fair price to offer? The goals of your life have to be defined in order for you to see their value too. You won't fight for what you don't value; you won't pay a high price for things you don't believe in. Remind yourself often why you're doing what you're doing.

Do Not Be Satisfied with Partial Victories: Assess the area in which you are winning, and then ask: "How can I do this even better?" In our ministry, we are intentional about celebrating successes, but we refuse to stay there for too long. We are thankful for our victories, but we know we have other victories that need to be won. Let your small victories become motivators in your life, but remain tenacious until you see your goals all the way to completion.

Be In It Forever: Like a recovering alcoholic, the obstacles of your life, even though they were defeated, will remain hiding in a corner waiting for an opportunity to assault you yet again. Don't be deceived by your wins; sometimes they can become your biggest enemy. The complacency derived from a partial victory can become a trap in the future. Lock into the long term, and let your legacy be defined by a lifetime of commitment rather than a moment of celebration.

Don't Be Defined by Others: Stop allowing someone who has no true relational investment in you to tell you what areas in which you do or do not excel. When they begin to espouse their opinion (which is usually a negative one), quickly and politely correct them. You can do almost anything you set your mind on. There will always be someone who has tried something similar to what you're trying and failed. Their story is not your story; their failure is not your failure. People are quick to define others. They say things like: "I tried that before," or "That can't be done," but your dream belongs to you because nobody will believe in it the way you do. Your dream is not everyone else's dream and that's okay. Others' definitions of you and your aspirations can sometimes be helpful, but they can also be harmful. Choose your mentors carefully. Your dream is your responsibility and nobody else's!

Chapter 6: The Setback

We've all had that not-so-pleasant experience. You know, the one you knew was a possibility, but hoped would never happen. It's been called a plateau, the wall, the glass ceiling—or worse, the setback. It's when you're moving full steam ahead, all cylinders firing perfectly, and then suddenly progress comes to a screeching halt. Setbacks are as normal in the growth patterns of life as the daily sunrise and sunset. You may have been privileged to avoid many things, but you will seldom be fortunate enough to avoid ever having some sort of setback.

Most every athlete has experienced the frustration of a strained muscle or training injury that prolonged their progress or even ended their career. All the hours of hard work and training now appeared pointless, and their future became uncertain. Sometimes we see athletes bounce back from serious injury and fully recover. Others are never able to completely heal and, sadly, realize their athletic future is over.

The majority of businesses have had setbacks too, some of which can become so frustrating that the future of the business becomes unclear. Whether due to a corporate merger, changing economic trends, or maybe even a scandal in the boardroom, what used to be wildly successful is now only a distant memory. Business setbacks require major planning and sometimes corporate restructure so the company becomes profitable once again.

Even marriages are not immune to setbacks. Lack of communication or trust issues can undermine a relationship. Over time as a couple begins to evolve, it's possible for the two to begin to drift apart rather than grow closer. We all know people who have walked down the painful road of divorce. If not corrected, marital setbacks can be devastating and impact the lives of the whole family.

These are just a few of the possible areas where reversals can occur; in fact, they can pop up in any area of your life where you are seeking growth and development. They can be discouraging, and, in some cases, detrimental to future growth. Trouble can become a force of its own, and if not handled properly, can root itself in our lives as our very own giant. This particular giant is very intimidating, as we realize that what enabled us to be successful in the past no longer works now. This discouragement coupled with the uncertainty of how to move forward can create a frustration that builds anxiety and disillusionment.

Growth during Setback

As hard as it may be, a setback doesn't have to end bad; in fact, it can lead to incredible growth. The pause button on life helps us consider different routes to get to our desired destination. During seasons of success we are often moving so quickly that it is easy to miss opportunities for improvement. If our own self-development was a continuous experience of comfort and ease, we would never have the motivation to change anything. We would be content to leave well enough alone and never achieve higher levels than those we'd already experienced. Sometimes our greatest successes are born from our most painful setbacks.

Sometimes our greatest successes are born from our most painful setbacks.

There is a famous proverb which says necessity is the mother of invention. This is profoundly true. Most every successful invention was created in order to solve some sort of problem. Before the plate was invented, I imagine eating a meal was messy and inconvenient. Somewhere along the line, someone had the genius idea to create something to hold food so each person could have their own portion. The plate was born! Were it not for the problem of messy food, there would be no need for the invention that has now made our lives so much better.

In our setback seasons, we are forced to think about how to get past the position we are in. Though it may be difficult or even painful, some of our best ideas can be generated while trying to move beyond our frustration. The desire for personal relief can birth the means to

kill the giant.

accomplish our hardest goals. The need to recalibrate our vision and rethink our goals can be blurred by success, but setbacks wake us up to see the need for change.

Throughout history there are numerous examples of people who faced setbacks but were able to overcome them. We've seen wounded and discouraged war heroes who refused to give up and won monumental battles. Other have overcome physical adversities and sickness and then went on to become highly successful. Businesses have suffered great loss but bounce back and become innovators in their fields. Of all the examples of successfully handling the setback, few can compare to the biblical story of Joseph.

Some of our best ideas can be generated while trying to move beyond our frustration.

Joseph's Many Setbacks

Joseph was a young man and his father's favorite. His father loved him so much that he gave him a colorful coat that identified him as "Daddy's special boy." Can you imagine the seething hatred Joseph's brothers felt as they watched him walking around, proudly displaying the trophy of his father's love? We get a glimpse of this intense sibling rivalry as we read the scriptural account.

Now Israel loved Joseph more than all his children, because he was the son of his old age. Also he made him a tunic of many colors. But when

Chapter 6: The Setback

his brothers saw that their father loved him more
than all his brothers, they hated him and could not
speak peaceably to him (Genesis 37:3-4).

Make no mistake, these boys hated Joseph—and
it wasn't just a passive-aggressive rage either. They
displayed outright nasty behavior towards Joseph. They
were so jealous of him that they would not even speak
to him as a brother, but spoke to him like they would a
contentious rival. Joseph grew up as Daddy's favorite, but
to make things even worse, God gave Joseph ambitious
dreams for the future.

Now Joseph had a dream, and he told it to his
brothers; and they hated him even more. So he
said to them, "Please hear this dream which I have
dreamed: There we were, binding sheaves in the
field. Then behold, my sheaf arose and also stood
upright; and indeed your sheaves stood all around
and bowed down to my sheaf." And his brothers
said to him, "Shall you indeed reign over us? Or
shall you indeed have dominion over us?" So they
hated him even more for his dreams and for his
words (Genesis 37:5-8).

The hatred the brothers had against Joseph from his
birth was now getting even worse. Not only did Joseph
have a dream about his superiority, he actually had the
nerve to tell his brothers the details of the dream. As you
can see from their response, this didn't gloss over any
of their rage against him. Just when the confrontation
appeared to be at its peak, things got more heated.

Then he dreamed still another dream and told it
to his brothers, and said, "Look, I have dreamed
another dream. And this time, the sun, the moon,
and the eleven stars bowed down to me." So
he told it to his father and his brothers; and his
father rebuked him and said to him, "What is this
dream that you have dreamed? Shall your mother
and I and your brothers indeed come to bow
down to the earth before you?" And his brothers
envied him, but his father kept the matter in mind
(Genesis 37:9-11).

Now, Joseph's perceived air of superiority extended
beyond being better than his brothers. His latest dream
had even his own parents bowing down to him. These
dreams would prove to be from the Lord, but his brothers
didn't care about that. They were so jealous that they
couldn't see the hand of God on their little brother. When
you begin to take steps toward greater achievement in
your life, opposition will come. Joseph didn't need a
cheering squad to fulfill his purpose, and neither do you!

Joseph didn't need a cheering
squad to fulfill his purpose, and
neither do you!

Joseph's brothers weren't content to simply ridicule
or ostracize their brother; they wanted him completely
gone. They didn't want to reason with him or try to
convince him to change. Their agenda was to delete him
and his memory altogether. This led to a meeting of the

Chapter 6: The Setback

minds between the brothers that ended up in an ill fate for the younger sibling. The boy's father, Israel, sent Joseph to check on his brothers, who were moving the family livestock to various places for feeding. When they saw Joseph coming, their seething rage got the best of them and they came up with a plan.

> Now when they saw him afar off, even before he came near them, they conspired against him to kill him. Then they said to one another, "Look, this dreamer is coming! Come therefore, let us now kill him and cast him into some pit; and we shall say, 'Some wild beast has devoured him.' We shall see what will become of his dreams!" But Reuben heard it, and he delivered him out of their hands, and said, "Let us not kill him." And Reuben said to them, "Shed no blood, but cast him into this pit which is in the wilderness, and do not lay a hand on him"—that he might deliver him out of their hands, and bring him back to his father. So it came to pass, when Joseph had come to his brothers, that they stripped Joseph of his tunic, the tunic of many colors that was on him. Then they took him and cast him into a pit. And the pit was empty; there was no water in it (Genesis 37:18-24).

These boys had definitely crossed the line beyond sibling rivalry, and had now actively assaulted their youngest brother. They had had enough of his haughty behavior and lofty dreams. They were tired of trying to gain their father's approval by competing with someone they knew they could never beat. Their anger took over and put into motion a series of events they could never have imagined possible. As they now contemplated what to do with the young man, they saw some slave traders approaching from a distance. As they came closer, the brothers decided to sell young Joseph as a slave.

> Then Midianite traders passed by; so the brothers pulled Joseph up and lifted him out of the pit, and sold him to the Ishmaelites for twenty shekels of silver. And they took Joseph to Egypt (Genesis 37:28).

As we read this, it is hard to believe that people, let alone family members, could be capable of such behavior. When people begin to see your success, there will always be some who will be consumed with jealousy. There are always people who will want to keep you on their level rather than celebrating as you move to your next level. Joseph's brothers could only see him as the kid brother, the one who may have been a tattletale, Daddy's annoying little favorite.

There are always people who will want to keep you on their level rather than celebrating as you move to your next level.

We all want support and encouragement, but we cannot allow our future to hinge on what others think or say about us. I believe the moment Joseph was being hoisted out of the pit to be sold as a slave was a defining moment for him.

Chapter 6: The Setback

His brothers would not determine his future; a pit would not decide his fate; a group of slave traders could not undermine his destiny. Talk about a setback! Joseph was having a serious setback, however, his attitude in that moment of truth would determine whether he would rise or fall.

I have no doubt that Joseph was upset, angry, and disappointed by the actions of his brothers. Though he was confused and hurt, he did not allow bitterness to take over and begin to own him. We know this because of the great success he had in the future. One thing is for certain: When a person is consumed by bitterness, their ability to succeed is greatly diminished.

> When a person is consumed by bitterness, their ability to succeed is greatly diminished.

If Joseph would have been consumed by bitterness it would have affected his judgment and his future relationships, but most of all, it would have undermined his faith. Like the giants of old, bitterness during a time of trial can become a weight (or a shackle) around the neck. The weight doesn't become more manageable over time; it only gets heavier as time progresses. The more one thinks about how they've been wronged, the more bitter they can become.

Life as a Slave

Undoubtedly, Joseph wasn't happy about this terrible turn of events, but he was able to get past it and stay focused on his future. As Joseph was taken to Egypt, he was sold to an officer of Pharaoh who was a captain of the guard, a man named Potiphar. Even though he had been taken against his will, Joseph worked hard and was soon recognized as a model servant, one loved by Potiphar.

Potiphar not only liked Joseph, but also trusted him greatly. Joseph was soon put in charge of the everyday operations of the household, and eventually was given the responsibility of managing Potiphar's personal finances. Everything seemed to be going well. In fact, it could be said that Joseph's life had taken a drastic turn for the better. This was true for a while, but eventually Joseph would suffer yet another defeat.

Joseph's master, Potiphar, had responsibilities that were demanding which most likely required him to spend a great deal of time away from home. He may have been overworked and stressed out, and most likely showed some signs of that at home too. While Potiphar was consumed with his workload and its stress, Joseph was holding down the fort, maintaining a constant presence of capable family care and management.

Joseph had Potiphar's attention and their relationship grew stronger, as Joseph was trusted with more and more responsibility. Joseph not only blessed the home by his dedication and commitment, but was highly favored by God, which, in turn, became a blessing upon Potiphar's home. Joseph gained not only Potiphar's attention, but that of Potiphar's wife.

Chapter 6: The Setback

> Now Joseph was handsome in form and appearance. And it came to pass after these things that his master's wife cast longing eyes on Joseph, and she said, "Lie with me" (Genesis 39:6b-7).

Joseph's hard work and attention to detail caused Potiphar's wife to be attracted to him. This unwanted attention from his master's wife would prove to be a problem for Joseph and his relationship with Potiphar. Joseph continually denied her requests, but she persisted and refused to quit. Potiphar was a wealthy man, and his wife was most likely used to getting what she wanted. The denial of her advances toward Joseph angered her, so she retaliated.

Up to this point, Joseph's position in Potiphar's house had allowed him to enjoy the status he probably felt he deserved. For the first time in his life he was respected, honored, and appreciated. The advances from Potiphar's wife were more than inconvenient. I'm guessing he could see the handwriting on the wall. Joseph knew that this problem was coming to a head and he would have to handle himself very carefully in order to keep his preferred status within Potiphar's home.

There's an old saying: "You can't have your cake and eat it too." This means you can't have everything your own way. Joseph's integrity was about to be put to the test, and the outcome would be far less than favorable. Joseph was about to experience yet another setback, and this time it would cost him much more than a short stay in a pit.

But it happened about this time, when Joseph went into the house to do his work, and none of the men of the house was inside, that she caught him by his garment, saying, "Lie with me." But he left his garment in her hand, and fled and ran outside. And so it was, when she saw that he had left his garment in her hand and fled outside, that she called to the men of her house and spoke to them, saying, "See, he has brought in to us a Hebrew to mock us. He came in to me to lie with me, and I cried out with a loud voice. And it happened, when he heard that I lifted my voice and cried out, that he left his garment with me, and fled and went outside" (Genesis 39:11-15).

Joseph's problem with the wife of his master didn't go away; it escalated to the point that she forced herself on him. Joseph made the right moral decision, but this didn't stop Potiphar's sinful wife from fabricating a lie: both to cover her mistake and get Joseph into trouble. This woman's actions proved her to be not only sinful, but willing to ruin the lives of anyone necessary to seek her own vindication.

From this we learn that even though we are making good decisions and taking the moral high ground, it is still possible to experience setbacks. In fact, we can still be mistreated, harassed, and even slandered while we are making good choices. I've seen many people in my years of ministry who have become exhausted doing the so-called "right thing." They try to do right but don't seem to have a good return on their investment. If we are doing the right thing we sometimes make the mistake of thinking we should always be rewarded. The fact is that our reward may be delayed or may never appear at all.

After many years of faithfulness to Potiphar, Joseph's reward was pulled right out from under him. From Joseph's perspective, it looked like all the time he had spent working so selflessly was rendered pointless. In one moment, his unblemished record of integrity was turned into public humiliation—humiliation he did not deserve in the least.

From Bad to Worse

It's one thing to have such an accusation, but it is another entirely to be prosecuted because of it. Potiphar was a man of power, and it certainly appears that his orders carried a lot of influence. Without a trial or legal representation, and with no one to defend his integrity, Joseph was immediately thrown into prison.

> So it was, when his master heard the words which his wife spoke to him, saying, "Your servant did to me after this manner," that his anger was aroused. Then Joseph's master took him and put him into the prison, a place where the king's prisoners were confined. And he was there in the prison (Genesis 39:19-20).

Talk about a setback! Even as a lowly slave, Joseph had still been able to enjoy the comforts of a nice home and the respect of a household that trusted him. Now all of this was gone. Instead of the expensive artwork and paintings of a rich man's home, Joseph's scenery had been minimized to the four walls of a prison cell.

Joseph started out being loved by his father, only to be hated by his brothers. He was thrown into a pit to become a slave. He was then acquired by a wealthy man and promoted within his home. Now, once again, he was experiencing defeat as he was thrown into prison for something he didn't do. If there was a way to graph the emotional high points and low points of Joseph's life, it would look much like the EKG printout from a cardiologist's screening.

Just when Joseph was getting ahead and making strides towards success, he once again suffered a severe emotional blow. His feelings of peace and blessing were quickly erased and overcome by rejection and unfairness. Most of us experience this cycle in life to some degree.

There have been times in my life when I felt like I was on top of the world. There have been other times when it seemed like the world was on top of me. These feelings are not unique to any one individual, but are common to all. Even Jesus experienced this.

Jesus performed incredible miracles and then was ridiculed by those who were threatened by Him or misunderstood His intentions. One evening He was enjoying a wonderful Passover dinner with His followers, only to be betrayed by one within His own ranks. His own disciples celebrated His powerful resurrection, but later experienced dark and painful seasons of persecution and even martyrdom. Setbacks are erratic and can be painful and unpredictable, but one thing we can predict is that nobody is exempt!

The feelings of isolation during a setback can be very intense and all too real. We can be made to feel as if our setback is so unique that no one else has ever experienced anything like it before. We can also feel like no one understands or even cares. Remember, our feelings are often misleading and are seldom completely accurate when compared to the realities we are facing. We cannot allow our feelings to be the deciding factor of our actions. Sometimes our actions have to stand completely alone— apart from the weight of how we feel. Even though Joseph had a lot of mixed emotions while locked up in the dark and lonely prison cell of ancient Egypt, he was able to manage his troubles by forcing his actions to respond to his faith.

Sometimes our actions have to stand completely alone-apart from the weight of how we feel.

Joseph was backed up against the wall. He was in a position he didn't want to be in—and there was nothing he could do about it. All alone and forgotten by people, Joseph had a choice to make. He could allow this problem to alienate him from God, or he could use this as an opportunity to draw closer to the Lord. Joseph made a decision to keep being faithful and not allow bitterness to consume him.

> But the Lord was with Joseph and showed him mercy, and He gave him favor in the sight of the keeper of the prison. And the keeper of the

prison committed to Joseph's hand all the prisoners who were in the prison; whatever they did there, it was his doing. The keeper of the prison did not look into anything that was under Joseph's authority, because the Lord was with him; and whatever he did, the Lord made it prosper (Genesis 39:21-23).

We see an absolute in the life of Joseph: he dedicated himself to consistent excellence and refused to become bitter. Even in prison, Joseph was promoted to a place of leadership. We know this because the keeper of the prison had incredible trust in him. Trust is never given; it is always earned. The keeper of the prison saw consistency in Joseph's life, and that caused him to put even his own job at risk in order to promote him. Verse 23 reminds us that the keeper didn't even look into anything over which Joseph was in charge. Now that's trust!

Never allow a lack of vision today to steal the hope you have for tomorrow.

If you've ever had the experience of teaching your kids to drive, you know how challenging that can be. It will really teach you how to pray more effectively! My three kids all have very different personalities, and as such, the experience of teaching them this important life skill was unique to each. My daughter, who is my oldest, is very introverted and shy. She drove just like her personality. She often wanted to stop right in the middle of a road to wave ahead other waiting motorists. My

Chapter 6: The Setback

oldest son is a full-steam-ahead type in almost anything. Whether he knows what he's doing or not, he'll fool you into believing he's an expert. His driving was marked with overconfidence and many "near misses," as he was trying to prove his mastery in uncharted waters. My youngest, who is actually learning to drive now, is different than the other two. His driving is careful and calculated, much like his perfectionist and analytical personality.

The driving lessons all have the same objective with each of the three, that eventually they would be driving on their own without any supervision whatsoever. With this end in mind, however, I would not allow them to start that way. They started with me in the vehicle, micromanaging everything they did. Everything from braking to the use of turn signals, to observing traffic laws. I interjected constantly as the new drivers headed onto the open road. As time progressed, my guidance became less and less frequent as they learned to make decisions on their own. After proving themselves capable of managing the vehicle safely by passing the test, they finally had the ability to drive solo.

It's not that God is prepping us to handle life all alone. We know that He's always with us. However, every situation in life is a learning experience and helps us become better and more capable as people of faith. There are experiences I have gone through that have prepared me for my present circumstances. Without the benefit of past experience, I would be lost in the issues of today. God allows the hindrances of life to be more than just teaching exercises. They are powerfully used to build us and make our faith stronger each day.

Pit to Palace

Joseph was a work in progress, just like we are. Joseph's faith in God was stronger in the prison than it was when he was in the pit. In the pit, he was just getting started on an amazing journey that would lead to him to his destination. As he saw God's hand working in his life from the pit to Potiphar's house, and now to the prison, Joseph's faith was able to sustain him, even in the moments that seemed unfair.

Your setback today isn't because God forgot you, it's because God believes in you!

We like to reflect on Joseph in his glory days. We remember him as the second in command, second only to the Pharaoh of Egypt. Remember though, when Joseph was in the pit, he had no vantage point that would allow him to see the palace. Never allow a lack of vision today to steal the hope you have for tomorrow. It's important to stay faithful, grounded, committed, and focused in times of pain. These qualities will enable you to make it past the dark places and experience the blessings on the other side.

Your setbacks may have been so devastating that you allowed yourself to completely give up. Joseph could have easily fallen into this mindset himself. It's hard to stay focused and full of faith and hope when cast

Chapter 6: The Setback

into a deep, dark pit by your own family members. His glimmer of hope was promptly crushed when out of the pit, he was whisked away into the grip of an Egyptian slave master. When you see these setbacks as a means of preparation and growth for faith, you soon realize God was allowing these things to happen because He had big plans for Joseph. Your setback today isn't because God forgot you, it's because God believes in you!

The depth of your setback can determine the magnitude of your comeback.

Joseph experienced deep pain, like the hatred from the brothers that were supposed to love him. He knew the pain that came with the injustice of slavery. He also knew what it was to be framed and then convicted for a crime he did not commit. This deep pain though, would provide a powerful foundation for his next destination. In fact, the depth of your setback can determine the magnitude of your comeback. Joseph might have been down, but he was definitely not out!

While in prison, Joseph interpreted the dreams of two different prisoners. The interpretations of those dreams proved to be true. One of the prisoners was restored to his previous position prior to being incarcerated. This man, the personal butler to the Pharaoh, would later become instrumental in Joseph's eventual release and promotion.

Pharaoh had two dreams that troubled him, so much so that he was losing sleep and becoming a bit irrational about trying to determine the meaning of them. After a long search for someone to interpret the dream, Pharaoh's butler remembered the Hebrew prisoner who had interpreted his dream previously. Joseph was called from the prison to make an appearance before the leader of the nation.

> Your pain can blind you from
> seeing past your now, but your
> faith can help you hold on until
> you see your tomorrow.

God gave Joseph the interpretation of the dreams, and in short order, he was promoted over the land and the people of Egypt. From a bullied brother to slave and then prisoner, Joseph was now wearing the signet ring of the Egyptian Pharaoh. Nobody could have ever known that this would happen, but it was God's plan all along.

Never doubt the plans God has for you. You can't see them now, but believe me, He does. Your pain can blind you from seeing past your now, but your faith can help you hold on until you see your tomorrow. Joseph went from pit to promise, from prison to palace, and from pushed aside to promoted, but it was not easy. God's big plans require people's big faith. If you are in a setback, hold on, keep being faithful; God always has the final word.

One of the things that always seems to stand out in this story is the fact that there is no outcry from the public about Joseph's promotion. Remember, he was a Hebrew, he was a slave, and he was a convicted (innocently) sex offender. However, when Pharaoh rewarded him—even over his own people—with great wealth and position, it seems as if everyone forgot who he was. How is this possible? Maybe the gifting and demeanor of Joseph was so convincing that people forgot about what or who he used to be. God's promotion is so powerful that it can heal even the deepest pain from your past!

The insecurities of who you used to be are dwarfed by who you are now.

When God steps into your life and begins to push you into places bigger than you thought possible, somehow the insecurities of who you used to be are dwarfed by who you are now. The setback is never welcomed, but the growth that happens during the setback is invaluable. Anyone who has blazed a new path, set a new record, or pursued a big dream has experienced trial and difficulty. The setback can either make you or break you. Refuse to be defined by your setbacks; instead be defined by your comebacks! You may be only one push away from your breakthrough moment. In the next chapter, we will look at reviving the dream that has dried up and appears to be no longer valid.

6: The Setback
Action Points

Embrace the Setback: Think of some practical ways to use your current problem to your advantage; sometimes the opportunity to recalibrate where you are is the catalyst you need to advance quickly. You might as well understand that you cannot insulate yourself from ever having a setback. This will help you move quickly from the "Woe is me" mentality to the "How can I fix this?" one instead. This becomes very important because spending time bemoaning your pain never moves you forward. Time wasted in complaining about your reality will never change it. Time spent in adjusting and changing will shorten the season of the setback and help you gain the needed experience while in it.

Never Allow Opposition to Deter You: Determine the things that are opposing your success now. Think of some ways you can overcome those specific deterrents, even if it may take you a while. For example, if a lack of money is your deterrent, think of how you can produce additional income or find ways to cut spending. If people quit every time they ran into an obstacle, most everything we know today would not exist. People who have successful businesses will tell you that they've done a lot of things wrong along the way and have paid dearly for their mistakes. But they understand the power of learning from their mistakes, and those mistakes should not be allowed to stop them. There's a difference between sound advice and counsel, and just plain old negativity. Be careful to discern the difference; never allow the negativity of others keep you from your purpose.

Know That It Is Worth It in the End: Say this over your life right now: "I am in this to the end" and "I will not quit until I succeed." The blessing of Joseph's success quickly dissolved the pain of his past. In fact, he later shared with his brothers that they need not be sorry for how they treated him because he could now see God's hand in those events.

> But now, do not therefore be grieved or angry with yourselves because you sold me here; for God sent me before you to preserve life. For these two years the famine has been in the land, and there are still five years in which there will be neither plowing nor harvesting. And God sent me before you to preserve a posterity for you in the earth, and to save your lives by a great deliverance. So now it was not you who sent me here, but God; and He has made me a father to Pharaoh, and lord of all his house, and a ruler throughout all the land of Egypt (Genesis 45:5-8).

The setback is always unpleasant at the time you experience it, but it is necessary for position and strength for what may prove to be your greatest comeback!

Chapter 7: Never Stop Dreaming

Have you ever known someone who gave up on their dream? Maybe they wanted to be an inventor or a scientist, but somewhere along the way the dream ceased to exist. I think all of us understand this to one degree or another. One guy wonders what it would have been like to be a professional ball player, while a lady daydreams about what it would have been like to be a famous Hollywood actress. These are very common dreams, but the question I'm asking is deeper. I'm not talking about fantasizing about what could have been, but about quitting on what should have been.

I have a friend we'll call Tom. Tom was truly destined to be a world-changer. I remember him in high school. He had a charm about him that was nothing less than magnetic. In our public speaking class, he was the guy who spoke effortlessly about most any subject in front of the class. He did so with such style and sense of humor that he had the whole class laughing and interacting each time he spoke. He was truly naturally gifted in front of people. We all knew that he would someday end up in politics, ministry, or on the motivational speaking circuit.

kill the giant.

As time progressed, Tom's gift became more and more apparent. He was captain of the debate team, a leader in his youth group, and was the center of attention at every social event. Tom often talked about his future and the fact that he knew he would really make a mark on the world in some way. He had begun to narrow down his interests and decided that politics would be his future. Like most guys that age, another one of his interests had to do with young ladies. He began to date one of the girls in our school and they really looked like a match made in heaven. I remember the running joke around school was their nicknames; many called him "Governor" while she was "First Lady."

I lost track of Tom after high school. I got involved in my own life like everyone else, but I often wondered what happened to him. I made a few contacts through social media and found out that things didn't turn out the way most had expected for Tom. He and his girlfriend from high school broke up and he met another girl. This girl became pregnant and Tom was forced to quit college to support his new family. Instead of pursuing politics, Tom was biding his time grinding it out working at an out-of-state retail store.

When I initially heard about this, I was shocked. How could this happen? Tom was dripping with natural talent, but now working shift work at a local retailer. There was absolutely nothing wrong with that kind of work, but we really thought he was well on his way to making waves in the political arena. It would have been easy to blame this on his girlfriend or his bad decisions. The sad thing is not the actual circumstances that led him to that place, but the fact that Tom's dream ceased to exist.

Reviving the Dream

The question now becomes this: Is it possible to resuscitate a dream that has expired? I want to tell you that one hundred percent, definitely, and without hesitation, the answer to that question is: a dream can absolutely be revived! The dream can die with the person, but if the person still lives, the dream can live on. In Tom's case, the dream may no longer be on a linear path. We thought he would graduate and then get a degree in political science, do some volunteer work, and then go on to win elections—now this wasn't going to happen. The path would surely be different, but the dream could remain unchanged.

Anybody can do easy things; only champions can do hard things.

Don't ask yourself this: "Can the dream still happen?" Instead, ask this: "How can the dream still happen?" Don't think you can no longer live your dream; find out how your dream can be fulfilled, and how to get there. This is not easy, but remember that anybody can do easy things; only champions can do hard things.

Think about these questions: *Is my dream worth reviving?* If it is, transition from an *if* way of thinking to a *how* way of thinking. You can *if* yourself until

159

kill the giant.

you are absolutely crazy. So do not waste time on *ifs:*
If I had the money, or *if I had the time*, or *if I had the*
education. Revive the dream. A *how* approach already
assumes possibility, it just needs the framework of a plan.
Sometimes our giant isn't the size of the dream itself, it's
the doubt that the dream can ever live again that needs to
be overcome.

Failure is not an option.

You have to believe in the plan and work it until
you succeed. I shared this concept in my last book, *The*
Left-Handed Warrior. Always remember: failure is not
an option. You may fail, and most likely you will fail
many times, but "fail" is a verb. "Failure" is an identity.
If you're not failing, you're probably not working hard
enough. Any successful person would be able to share a
very long list of things they did wrong along the way to
their success. If failure stopped them, they never would
have achieved success, and the dream would have died.

As a teenager, like most, I highly anticipated the day I
would get my first car. My sights were much higher than
the depth of my parent's bank account. In fact, much to
my dismay, they required me to pay for half the cost of
the car. I worked for many hours at summer jobs, trying
to raise the money to make that all important purchase.
I dreamed of the classic hot rod car, but ended up with a
1979 Toyota Celica instead.

It was no hot rod for sure, but it was transportation
and I was proud to have it. The only issue I had was the

car was a stick shift and I had only driven vehicles with an automatic transmission. It was almost like learning to drive all over again. My poor dad had spent hours teaching me to drive, and now he had to teach me how to handle a standard transmission. It seemed like a pretty steep learning curve, and it took me quite a while to finally be comfortable driving.

On multiple occasions, I accidentally shifted down instead of up. The car slowed quickly and revved with incredible intensity. I honestly don't know how that transmission survived my training period. There were also times when I let out the clutch too quickly and the car stalled; my all-time favorite was coming to a red light on a steep incline. There were times when I wanted to quit; I wanted to sell the car, trade the car, take a taxi to school every day—anything other than force myself to learn how to drive the elusive and difficult stick shift. However, my desire to be able to drive my very own vehicle kept me motivated to stay the course.

The reward of success is always
worth the pain of failing
along the way.

After many unsuccessful excursions, tense exchanges with my dad, and a whole lot of frustration, I was finally able to handle the open road with a fairly strong degree of confidence. It wasn't easy to get there, but the reward of success is always worth the pain of failing along the way. To have given up because of my uneasiness and frustration would have nullified all the hard work I had gone through raising funds, not to mention the money my parents had spent. If I added my hours of practice on top of that, it was easy to see that quitting was not a sensible option.

The path of least resistance may seem like the easiest way, but it is usually not the most rewarding. Like you, I've seen countless people start things with the stage presence of an Atlas rocket launch, only to quit as soon as they faced discouragement and the reality of the hard work this new endeavor would require.

Your dream will not be fulfilled because of someone else, but because of you.

The dream has to remain stronger than the opposition to the dream. The things we find highly rewarding are the things we will invest in heavily, and not only ride out, but overcome. Discouragement that threatens the dream along the way will be cast aside. If you don't highly value your dream, you should give up on it now because it isn't really a dream. Just like nobody cares for your personal things the way you do, nobody understands and cares for your dream the way you do. If your dream is to be achieved, it is because you own it, believe in it, and work for it like nobody else will. Your dream will not be fulfilled because of someone else, but because of you.

Things die when they no longer have the ability to sustain life. Whether it be a plant, animal, person, or any other living thing, there are certain components necessary for life to continue to exist and be sustained. If a dream is lacking in one or more areas and is not corrected, it's only a matter of time before the dream dies.

The Dream Is a Living Organism

Like any organism, a dream must be healthy and vibrant for it to last and eventually be fulfilled. **The first question you want to ask yourself is, "Is the dream healthy?"** It is possible to have dreams based on things that may be unrealistic or will not bear the best outcome in your life. For example, if I began to dream about being a professional football player, I know that considering my age and other factors, it probably wouldn't be the healthiest dream. I can already hear the thoughts of those reading this: *You can dream anything you want and it can happen.* Although I do believe in dreaming big, we do have to understand that sometimes our dream may be mistaken for a wish. A true dream is something you work for, something you believe in, and something you are so consumed with that it keeps you up at night. I don't know of many professional football teams looking for fifty-year-old players, so this could probably be better classified as a wish.

People have to understand that their desire is fueled by something they know needs to be done, *but that may not mean it needs to be done by them*. Early in my ministry I had a desire for missions. I often dreamed about what it would be like to live in the plains of eastern Africa and to travel around, preaching to villages that had never heard the gospel. What I later realized was that God would allow me to support missions as a pastor by raising funds and equipping people to go into the mission field. This was more than I could do as one person traveling to the field myself. Sometimes the dream we have is a great dream, but God is shaping that dream into something even bigger and far more impactful than we realize.

Another question is this: **Is the dream being properly nourished?** Like all living things, a dream must be fed in order to stay alive. A person has a limited capacity for survival without food and water. Your pets, plants, and anything else you may have that is living also needs vital life-giving nutrients in order to survive.

> Like all living things, a dream must be fed in order to stay alive.

A while back I began to notice that my yard was looking a little rough. My once plush, green grass was withered and dry. We live in Florida, so the heat is a constant challenge in trying to keep a nice-looking lawn. I was paying someone to come every month and apply fertilizer as well as weed and fungus control on my lawn. I was concerned about the health of my yard, so I decided to check my invoices to see if they were keeping their schedule. I found out that they had been coming out exactly as promised. Still concerned, I thought I would investigate a little further. I believed my grass was being watered enough, as I have an automatic timer for the irrigation system, but decided to check it anyway. As I looked over the scheduled watering times, I realized that somehow several areas of my yard were turned off completely. With a few clicks of the automatic timer, we were back in action. After just a few weeks of proper watering, my green grass was back. What happened? The grass was getting the needed nutrients from the fertilizer, but it did not have sufficient water to deliver those nutrients to the roots.

Feeding and nourishing our dream is very similar; we may have certain pieces in place that feed and encourage the fulfillment of our dream, but if there is a void in any area, the dream can begin to suffer. If you feel like your dream is stalling or just not coming together as fast as it should, you need to do a little investigating. A dream is fed in several ways:

Constantly Revisiting the Why: Why is your dream important? Why does your dream need to be fulfilled? Who is your dream for? How will things be improved because of your dream? If there is no *why*, you will eventually lose motivation because the cost of the dream will outweigh its purpose.

Finding Ways to Make It Happen: A big dream is never fulfilled easily, but if you want it badly enough there is usually a way to see it come to pass. Find others who have been successful in the area of your dream; learn from them. Read, study, and absorb teaching that will help you grow. The world is full of people, organizations, and businesses which fought hard to become successful. Search for the underlying principles that made them successful and begin to implement those keys in your strategy too.

A Healthy Understanding of the Word *No*: Most anyone who has been even moderately successful in their life will tell you that they had to endure their share of *nos* before they ever broke through to their *yes*. The word *no* needs to be understood as a seasonal term: What may be a *no* now may become a *yes* later. Additionally, a *no* from one person is not equal to a *no* from every person. Sometimes it's not that you're asking the wrong question. You may be asking the right question, but to the wrong person.

Is your dream being properly
cared for?

The third question is this: "Is your dream being properly cared for?" We have recently discovered the joy of being first-time grandparents. There is nothing else like it in the world. My wife and I have loved this little girl from before she was even born. We have even given ourselves special names: Pops and GiGi. We will spoil little Ember Jane like she's the only little girl in the world. As a newborn, she is completely helpless and depends on others for everything. Without the oversight and supervision from the adults in her life, she would not be able to live.

Chapter 7: Never Stop Dreaming

As little Ember Jane gets older, she will grow and begin to do some things on her own. She will be able to feed herself, clothe herself, and eventually grow up and become an adult woman. A dream operates in a similar way. When the dream first emerges, it is completely helpless and the level of care you must provide is exhausting. However, over time as the dream begins to grow it begins to stand on its own, and the type of care you give changes. In the early stages, your job is to support and encourage growth, and later your care changes into steering and helping the dream attain even greater levels.

A dream is proven successful according to its health, nourishment, and care. These three areas, though generalized, will move the dream from its inception to its realization. If any one of these three ingredients is missing, the dream is sure to fail. Take a few minutes to analyze your dream and see if any of these three areas could be improved upon to help jumpstart your dream into fruition.

Dream Assessment

There is a difference between a dream and an assignment. An assignment usually has a beginning and an end. When you were in school, the teacher assigned specific work to be done. Certain pages had to be read and possibly some questions had to be answered to be turned in the next day. This assignment had a specific purpose for a specific time period. Once completed, it was over. A dream is different; a dream may look similar to an assignment in the beginning, but a dream may never have a point of completion.

As an example, I have a friend who is a professional bass fisherman. This man fishes with some of the top fishermen in the world. He has been seen on television, written about fishing in magazines, and interviewed for various articles about the sport. He is doing very well and is considered one of the elite fishermen in the world. Being a professional fisherman was a childhood dream. When he was young, other kids were bouncing basketballs, playing video games, or eating snacks, but he was in his garage practicing his pitching (a specific casting technique) that would allow him to cast with pinpoint accuracy. He worked his whole life to get better and learn everything he could about the sport. Any time he could get on the water, you better believe he was out there honing his skill.

He began to fish competitively at an early age, and before long he was bringing home trophies and rising in the amateur ranks. Over time, this led to some key sponsorships. Eventually he earned his spot on the professional fishing circuit. It would be easy to think that he accomplished his dream and became a professional fisherman. This would be true, but in reality that would only be the completion of a self-assigned task. Here's why: his dream is ongoing. He still continues to fish and becomes better and better as he lives it out.

Chapter 7: Never Stop Dreaming

When we accomplish something, we usually celebrate and memorialize the event in some way. When we have a birthday, we have a party complete with a cake, gifts, and singing. We don't continue the celebration forever. It's an accomplishment, but once it's done, it's done. It's the same way with anniversaries, retirements, moving into a new home, and so on. A dream is different. Once you have achieved whatever level of success you were shooting for, the dream isn't over. It's just been born.

> The dream has to continue to be
> fueled or it can vanish into the
> distance as a faded memory.

My fisherman friend knows that for the dream to stay alive he has to continue growing on an upward trend. He does this by constantly studying the topography of the lakes he will fish and checking to see if there are areas that look like they may be holding the "big one." He interviews the locals to see if he can get any special "insider" information. He's always trying new lures, new techniques, and different equipment. He does this because the dream didn't cease to exist the moment he joined the tour. That was just when it began to live! A dream that sees success and accomplishment is worthy of celebration, but the dream has to continue to be fueled or it can vanish into the distance as a faded memory.

A statement I heard often as I was growing up was, "If it's not broke, don't fix it." While this may certainly apply to the bathroom toilet, the front door, or certain applications, this statement can become the kiss of death for your dream. A dream cannot live on its own; it has to be continually strengthened, redefined, and repurposed. History is full of corporate stories of companies who used to be at the top of their game in their chosen field, but their comfort became their downfall. When you are experiencing success, it is often hard to appreciate the necessity to continually work at becoming even better.

I'm sure you can think of many companies that used to exist, but are now no longer in business or only a shadow of their former glory. For some of these companies, their lack of continued success could be a reflection of market trends and changes outside their control. For many though, the problem is much easier to pinpoint and even easier to correct. Their lack of success has to do with their comfort in sitting at the top of their game. Success is a fickle beast; it can be enjoyable one minute, and flee away at breakneck speed the next. Success cannot be viewed as a moment, but a lifestyle or mindset. If our dream continues to live, it's because we have the mindset to continue to change and move as the need demands.

> The success story of today
> could easily become the story of
> failure tomorrow.

In our church ministry, we are always challenging ourselves to do better at the things we do. Our church has experienced great success with many community outreaches that draw thousands of people to our campus.

Chapter 7: Never Stop Dreaming

However, if we began to think that we have all the best ideas and all the best techniques, then we would never change. The success story of today could easily become the story of failure tomorrow. Companies that remain successful long-term are companies that continue to innovate. Top companies usually invest a large amount of their budget on research and development. They understand the necessity of continually growing the dream and never being lulled to sleep by a false sense of accomplishment.

Michelangelo is credited with saying that the greater danger for most of us comes not by setting our aim too high and falling short, but by setting our aim too low and achieving our mark. When we set our sights low, we have a better chance of success, but at the end of the day, what have we really accomplished? A dream keeps our passion alive; it becomes a source of motivation that moves us to improve. A dream helps define our *now* and keeps us on a steady path of improvement. When a dream begins to fade, it becomes distant and sickly. A sick dream is sometimes harder to resuscitate than fulfilling a dream that is overambitious.

There are no guarantees of
success as you move forward,
but quitting is a guarantee
of failure.

It's easy to fall into the trap of thinking: I've been trying this for years with no success. When you get bogged down and feeling that you have fallen short, it can be quite a hard blow to your motivation. The real question is this: Is this dream worth fighting for? If the answer to this question is yes, then you have to immediately shift your thinking. You have to reengineer your approach—regardless of any plan that failed in the past. There are no guarantees of success as you move forward, but quitting is a guarantee of failure.

Resurrection as God's Plan

What are God's thoughts about dreams being resuscitated? One of the greatest Bible stories of all times is about the resuscitation of life. In fact, it was the resurrection of a man who had been dead for four days. It painted a picture of a family with whom Jesus was very close. He had stayed with sisters Mary and Martha and their brother Lazarus many times. There came a time when Jesus was notified that Lazarus was sick. The messenger informed Jesus that Lazarus's sickness was life-threatening and that time was of the essence.

> Now Jesus loved Martha and her sister and Lazarus. So, when He heard that he was sick, He stayed two more days in the place where He was. Then after this He said to the disciples, "Let us go to Judea again" (John 11:5-7).

Did you catch that? Jesus stayed where He was for two days after hearing the news. Why would He do that? It seems to me that if a close friend was in a near-death situation, most people would drop everything and immediately run to that location. Jesus chose to intentionally stay and not respond with a physical visit until later. This tells us quite a bit about how God thinks.

1. God's timing is not the same as ours.

2. He sees things differently than the way we see them.

3. What we consider an emergency is not always considered as such by God.

Jesus wasn't saying *no* to Lazarus and his healing, but He was saying *yes* to an even greater miracle. Such a significant amount of time passed between Jesus hearing about Lazarus being sick and His later response that Lazarus passed away. As Jesus entered the city where Lazarus and the sisters lived, it became apparent that they weren't too happy with Jesus' lack of urgency over His arrival.

Sometimes a dream that is resurrected is more powerful than a dream in its original state.

What happened here? To them the dream was dead! The dream of Lazarus being miraculously healed, as they had seen Jesus do for others many times before, was now impossible. Their friendship didn't seem too important any longer. What about all the time the family had spent opening up their house and showing Jesus hospitality?

Could He not come quickly? What was so important that it kept Jesus from arriving in time to heal His friend, their brother, Lazarus, anyway?

The thing about a dream is this; sometimes a dream that is resurrected is more powerful than a dream in its original state. It is possible to get so dialed into where we are that our focus becomes misguided. There are times when we are pursuing something that is good, but we are just pursuing it the wrong way. Sometimes a relaunch of a business is more successful than the original one was. The original launch may have been good, but the relaunch comes from a perspective that has more experience and has seen success and failures. So although that first attempt was good, the next one carries the weight of "how-to," that in the right environment can make it even better. In the story of Lazarus, a miracle was coming, but this miracle would be far greater than a physical healing. This miracle would go down in history as one of the most notable of all time.

Now just for the record, I don't believe God is in the business of allowing people to die in order to prove a point. However, I do believe that God's purpose is so much higher than ours, that for us to completely understand His ways would be impossible. Sometimes the best thing for us is to allow our dream to die, not so it is forgotten, but so that it is resurrected in a state that far exceeds the original plan.

As Jesus approached the tomb, there were onlookers who had no clue about what they would soon witness.

Chapter 7: Never Stop Dreaming

Lazarus's body was already in a cave with a stone sealed over the entryway. This meant the funeral had already taken place and Jesus' appearance at this point was too little, too late. However, Jesus didn't allow the confusion and unbelief of the people to hinder His action. He continued to proceed with His plan. It was a plan all right—an incredible plan they would not soon forget. As we read on in the biblical account, the plan becomes clearer.

> Then Jesus, again groaning in Himself, came to the tomb. It was a cave, and a stone lay against it. Jesus said, "Take away the stone." Martha, the sister of him who was dead, said to Him, "Lord, by this time there is a stench, for he has been dead four days." Jesus said to her, "Did I not say to you that if you would believe you would see the glory of God?" Then they took away the stone from the place where the dead man was lying. And Jesus lifted up His eyes and said, "Father, I thank You that You have heard Me. And I know that You always hear Me, but because of the people who are standing by I said this, that they may believe that You sent Me." Now when He had said these things, He cried with a loud voice, "Lazarus, come forth!" And he who had died came out bound hand and foot with graveclothes, and his face was wrapped with a cloth. Jesus said to them, "Loose him, and let him go" (John 11:38-44).

The healing of the sick is always a life-changing and noteworthy miracle. This miracle, however, was in a completely different realm. This miracle included bringing someone back to life who had been dead for four days! So Jesus was on board with a miracle for Lazarus and his family. Jesus wanted the miracle to be bigger than the healing of sickness.

Listen to this takeaway: Sometimes your dream is not fulfilled and it isn't because it's too big; it's because it is not big enough! God had a miracle for Mary, Martha, and Lazarus, but this miracle far surpassed anything they had the audacity to request. In reality, the dream had never died, it had just taken on a form much bigger than anyone expected. Can your dream live again? Yes, your dream can live again, but if you are going to expend the energy to dream, at least dream big!

Sometimes your dream is not fulfilled and it isn't because it's too big; it's because it is not big enough!

Can you imagine the faces of the people when Lazarus walked out of that dark tomb? People who were shaking their heads and pursing their lips over the fact that Jesus arrived four days late were now in utter shock. When the stone was rolled away, people gasped that this unorthodox request was actually being entertained. Then Lazarus, the dead man, still wrapped in his graveclothes, came stumbling out of the open tomb. Now that is a true miracle, and a dream that is resuscitated! God is not afraid to revive a dream; He is not afraid to relaunch an idea; He is not unwilling to breathe life into something that appears to be dead. God is just looking for people who will stand, believe, and dare to keep dreaming.

For a man to be raised up from a sickbed is a powerful testimony indeed, but for a man to be raised from a grave site is much more powerful. The onlookers that day got more than they bargained for; it was something they would never forget. If they had any doubt about the power of Jesus, those doubts were crushed the day the dead man walked out of the tomb. Your dream can far surpass any expectation you may have for it. God may be telling you today: "It's time to kick it up a notch!"

God is just looking for people
who will stand, believe, and dare
to keep dreaming.

I began this chapter with a story about my friend, Tom. I mentioned that Tom had a bright future ahead of him, but sometimes things in our lives have a way of changing. Again, his current situation would not be deemed unsuccessful in any way, but his current situation is not a reflection of his childhood and adolescent dream. As we have discussed, dreams can be revived and resurrected. In Tom's case, his dream could absolutely be revitalized, but it would take a tremendous amount of work.

Dreams have a way of becoming more complicated over time. For Tom to regroup and relaunch his dream of pursuing politics, it would mean going back to school.

kill the giant.

It would also probably mean a physical move to a new location. It would also involve networking with a different circle of people and completely changing his thought patterns and way of functioning and doing business. Again, this doesn't mean it would be impossible; it just means it would be hard. Sometimes we look at our dream and think: To do this now would require so much. You are most likely correct, but I will tell you this: It usually doesn't get any easier. The longer you wait, the more complicated it becomes. There is no time like the present to get out there and begin doing what you have always wanted to do.

There is no time like the present
to get out there and begin
doing what you have always
wanted to do.

Have you been guilty of making repetitive excuses about why you never finished what you started? Do you envy others who are living out your dream, and take on guilt over what you should have done? Do you find yourself living in constant regret and wondering, "What if I would have done things differently?" Are you unhappy because you can't get past what could have been? If you find yourself in this scenario, it might be time to give some thought to resuscitating that old dream.

You are never too old or too far spent to have a dream. In fact, the Bible tells us that dreams are not reserved for the young, but they actually have a place for those who are older.

> And it shall come to pass afterward that I will pour out My Spirit on all flesh; your sons and your daughters shall prophesy, your old men shall dream dreams, your young men shall see visions (Joel 2:28).

Part of this prophecy is that *the old* will dream again! Regardless of your age or frustration level, you can obtain a dream or resurrect one that appears to be dead. My encouragement to you is that no matter what is trying to suppress your dream, go back to your core conviction. Always believe in your God and your dream—and no matter what, never stop dreaming!

7: Never Stop Dreaming
Action Points

Determine the Value of Your Dream: Make a mental or even a physical list of why your dream is so important. Refer to this list often. It will keep you grounded when nothing else will. By nature, you are made to fight for what is important. If you aren't willing to fight, that's an indicator that the dream is not part of your core conviction. If you can remain passive and let it die, the truth is that the dream isn't one you're truly passionate about. If, however, you are willing to fight and move forward at most any cost, it is an indicator that your passion and dream have intersected. Without this important intersection, a dream can never move forward. You will not advance anything you are not passionate about.

Find Your *Why*: If you don't really know the *why* of your dream, it might move forward in the short term, but it will soon sputter and die. *Why* are you working so hard? *Why* do you believe in this invention? *Why* does everyone need to have this product? These are examples of questions you need to ask in order to find your *why*. If you are pursuing your dream because you don't really know what else to do, it will prove to be an inadequate motivator in the long term. A dream consumes you, whereas a goal is simply a milestone you use to measure success. Never confuse the two. A dream needs a *why*. A goal only needs a definition.

Chapter 7: Never Stop Dreaming

Revisit Your *Why*: Finding your *why* is key, but then you have to remind yourself often, sometimes even daily, of what it is. My wife and I began our ministry because we were passionate about lost souls coming to know the Lord. Sometimes the struggle and frustration of ministry is all too real, but when we revisit our *why*, the adversity becomes a little more manageable. If I didn't have a clearly defined *why*, I would have quit a long time ago. The *why* becomes the foundation of everything you do. It's not a hobby or a temporary fad, but a core conviction, and an absolute of all that you are willing to sacrifice in your life.

Take the Boundaries Off Your Dream: Ask yourself this question, "How can I make my dream bigger?" A dream that is small isn't really a dream; it's just a thought. If you tightly bind your dream with boundaries that are too restrictive, you can easily suffocate it. Walt Disney didn't limit his dream to a scratch pad and some cartoon figures; his thinking far surpassed even those who were closest to him. I live in central Florida, and our entire culture here has been impacted by this one man and his limitless dream that refused to know any boundaries.

Face the Giant of Regret: It is never too late to pick up where you left off. The daunting task of restarting something you quit before can be overwhelming in itself. Once you get past the initial mental boundary of the restart, it is much easier to find your motivation as progress begins to follow. Regret will always lurk in the shadows. When you face regret head-on, you can completely disarm its power. Make a choice to stop living in regret and take back what is being taken from you! It's never acceptable to "cry over spilled milk." There may be something specific you can do to alleviate the regret of the past. Sometimes a simple apology or even attempting a new skill set can erase years of painful regret. Whatever will take care of it, find it and do it.

Chapter 8: The Final Answer

A few years ago, there was a popular game show known for the line: "Is that your final answer?" As contestants talked through their reasons for selecting a particular answer, they were always given an opportunity to change their mind before locking it in. While the contestants mulled that important question, they would invariably answer, "Yes, that's my final answer." This meant that there was no turning back. With the same degree of certainty as the pounding of a judge's gavel, the answer could not be changed. One of the keys to defeating opposition in your life is to fully understand how powerful the attitude of finality really is.

When something is determined as factual, there is no further reason to discuss what may or may not be. If you feel like you may have gained a few pounds, you might share that information with a few trusted friends. Other people may even make comments that you're looking a bit heavier. However, the true test of these claims can only be determined by stepping on a scale. If the scale reads higher, then yes, you have gained some weight. Guessing as to whether or not you may have gained weight now becomes irrelevant as the proof is in the numbers.

kill the giant.

When you are working toward defeating opposition, your attitude has to be one of finality. If you are unsure or wavering in any way about your objective, your chances of success are greatly diminished. Top level athletes don't just think they want to be the best. They absolutely know they want to be the best. A person who builds up a business from nothing to a multimillion-dollar status didn't get there by accident. They did it with certainty and unwavering resolve.

> Many times our goal isn't the problem. It's the way we are going about getting there that needs to be changed.

Sometimes we lose momentum and our attitude suffers when we realize our goals are going to take more work than we realized. Finality means we don't second-guess, we don't look back, we don't retreat, and we don't give up just because things get tough. This is more than just an intense attitude though; it's a mindset that says, "I will accomplish this one way or another." Many times our goal isn't the problem. It's the way we are going about getting there that needs to be changed. A mindset of finality realizes adjustments may be necessary along the way; but whatever those adjustments are, the goal remains the same.

Discouragement is a constant battle while traveling the road to success. We have to be very careful about the voices we allow into our lives. Some people are prone to negativity, and if you're not careful, they will influence you to aim lower than you otherwise would. On the other hand, there are some people who are absolutely brimming with positivity. I like these people. They make you feel like you're the greatest person in the world. If you're going to keep your head up and continue plowing forward, you have to restrict the negative influences and recruit the positive ones!

Negativity will cause you to begin to question your sense of resolve. You may have thoughts like: *What if they're right?* or *What if I really don't have what it takes?* Most of us will fight these feelings along the way on our own. We certainly don't need to add any outside negative influence to make it even worse. Finality understands that this is where you are going, and there will be no compromise or negotiation. This mindset becomes the voice that steers you and moves you when you are pressed on every side and your plans are constantly being threatened. The voice of finality is more than a simple feeling; it becomes a source of authority. With it, you gain the authority to succeed, win, work hard, and accomplish what you've set out to do.

A Lesson in Authority

As a young youth pastor, I was making plans to take a group of teens on our very first mission trip as a youth group. This was my first time leading a group of people out of the country. I was both excited and nervous at the same time. We would be working with a missionary in the Caribbean islands and doing some kid's ministry and evening crusades. The church I was in was relatively small, and like many church budgets, funds were tight.

We began to raise funds almost a year in advance. We did everything imaginable at that time: from selling cookbooks, T-shirts, car washes, bake sales, letter-writing campaigns (this was before social media was a thing!), yard work, and more. As the trip was soon approaching, we were very happy that the monies were finally raised. We had done extensive training with the group, had multiple parent meetings, talked through our strategy in the Caribbean, bought plane tickets, and had multiple prayer meetings. We were ready to go!

As we piled into the church van on our way to catch our flight, I can still remember the excitement of the kids and adults alike. Many of these people would be traveling outside the country for the very first time. It was a bit surreal as all the training, hard work, and planning had finally brought us to our departure. As we were driving, the conversations in the van were charged with excitement and enthusiasm over what it would be like in a foreign country. We were excited to travel, but more importantly, we were looking forward to using our gifts and talents to share the power of Jesus with hurting people.

We arrived at the busy airport and were dropped off to begin the process of checking in for departure. We had the usual group of ninety-pound teenage girls trying to lug a suitcase filled with their entire wardrobe, and the squeaky-voiced adolescent boys trying to prove how strong they were by carrying multiple bags. As we struggled up to the airline counter, we were filled with joy and enthusiasm as our long-awaited journey was finally becoming a reality.

After a long wait, as this was summer travel season, it was our group's turn to check in our luggage and get our boarding passes. I was at the front of the line and when I was called on, I promptly handed over a stack of papers with our flight information and all the kids' names meticulously spelled so as not create any problems at the counter. The airline agent looked at the stack of papers and began to thumb through them one at a time. Then she looked down at her computer screen for quite some time. The kids in the line were already restless; and with the now lengthy wait, they were beginning to chatter amongst themselves.

The airline agent looked up at me and then said, "I'll need to see passports for each passenger." My heart dropped. I knew I did not have passports for any of our passengers. At this time (the early 90s), travel to the Caribbean was handled differently than traveling intercontinentally. In fact, much to my amazement, they were just now transitioning over to a new policy which required Americans to use a passport for travel to the islands.

I had spoken with our resident missionary in the Caribbean about required documents and he had assured me that passports or visas were not required. A simple birth certificate would suffice, but nothing else was needed. That was the information that I was going on, but it sure didn't seem to be of much help now. When I explained all of this to the airline agent, she called for one of her supervisors. This man came out and explained that there had been a recent policy change, and yes, passports were required for travel to the Caribbean. As I spoke with him, I could feel the panic within me begin to rise. All this time, effort, and money was about to go down the drain, not to mention how stupid I was going to look when I had to explain to all the parents how they had wasted so much money for a trip that never happened!

As one of my adult leaders held my place in the line and continued to protest to the airline agent, I quickly darted for a payphone. (That's right a payphone. In the early 90s, cell phones were not really a thing yet!) As I grabbed the phone, I quickly called the missionary in the Caribbean and explained our dilemma. He was shocked to hear we were having trouble, and told me to give him a few minutes. He was going to make some phone calls. I gave him the number to the payphone I was on and hung up. I guarded that phone like my life depended on it, making sure nobody came within a five-foot radius.

I remember looking up and seeing my adult leader still arguing with the airline supervisor. The conversation seemed to be getting a little louder as this guy was getting more and more frustrated. I knew something had to give quickly, or we were going to be in big trouble. As I was waiting for a return call, I began to think to myself, *Who*

Chapter 8: The Final Answer

in the world would this missionary be able to call that could change the policy of an entire airline and allow thirty people to fly without proper documentation? It honestly seemed like a real longshot. I was already rehearsing my speech to the disappointed and disgruntled parents waiting at home.

```
Never accept no from someone
who doesn't have the authority
          to say yes.
```

About that time that the phone began to ring. I was so anxious that at the hint of the first sound I snatched the phone up and yelled, "Hello!" It was the missionary calling and he said, "Okay, I have it all worked out." He then proceeded to tell me that I needed to go to the ticket counter and give them a certain man's name. We'll call him Mr. Hernandez. He told me to write down his phone number and have anyone with a problem call Mr. Hernandez directly. I couldn't believe what I was hearing, nor could I believe that it would actually work.

I made a beeline back to the ticket counter and shared my newfound information with the meeting of what was now several supervisors still arguing with my adult leader. When I dropped that name, Mr. Hernandez, and then showed them that I had his private number, those supervisors looked at me like I had just pulled off the greatest heist of all time! Without any hesitation, luggage and boarding passes started flying like there was no tomorrow. To this day, I still don't know who

kill the giant.

this man was or what position he held, but whoever he was, he certainly had authority that those people respected greatly.

Takeaways

This story taught me several lessons firsthand. First of all, never accept *no* from someone who doesn't have the authority to say *yes*. How many people have told you that you couldn't achieve what you set out to do? Or that you weren't good enough to be who you wanted to be? We've all had those voices in our lives, but who gave them the authority to have the final word over our future? The truth is that they don't have that authority unless you give it to them. If you've ever had the great pleasure of door-to-door sales, you know that you typically hear a whole lot of *nos* before you ever get to a *yes*. The word *no* is sort of like the tamper-proof packaging on food. You have to work hard to get through it, but the end result is worth the effort.

In fact, I would say that if your objective is not met with any resistance, it probably isn't worth the effort. Anything worthwhile is not only difficult, but will almost always be met with some resistance. Mr. Hernandez had the final answer; his one word made all the negative responses, anxiety, and flaring tempers completely null and void. His authority made his word the *final word*. The resolve to succeed, achieve, and overcome will quiet the loud voices of opposition and kill the giant who would love to see you quit trying.

Chapter 8: The Final Answer

Another truth from this story is the lesson of perseverance. Some call it "thinking outside the box," meaning that you don't get trapped into one-dimensional thinking. In the airport, we could have very easily accepted the response that we were not allowed to travel, and jumped back into the van and headed home disappointed. However, thanks to some unruly teenagers, some headstrong parents, and a belligerent adult leader, we refused to simply accept the word *no*. Anytime you are on the path to success and victory, there will always be a giant standing in your path telling you *no*. A one-dimensional or passive approach will readily accept this as the only viable outcome. Successful people know that even if something is hard and not easily accessible, there is usually a way to get to your intended end.

If your objective is not met with
any resistance, it probably isn't
worth the effort.

In my last book, *The Left-Handed Warrior*, I wrote extensively on the subject of perseverance as one of the critical ingredients of success. From the standpoint of military strategy and warfare, soldiers are trained on the foundational premise that perseverance is not optional. Their training regimen includes endless hours of physical training, emotional and psychological: all designed to give them the tools necessary to persevere through the difficulties they would likely face. Even the Bible teaches the importance of perseverance.

kill the giant.

> But he who endures to the end shall be saved
> (Matthew 24:13).

Finally, the last lesson I learned from this story was that everyone has an opinion, but not all of them are helpful. The truth is, you had a destiny long before others had an opinion about you. From the biblical perspective alone, there are countless examples of people who assertively gave their opinions, but in the end, those opinions were completely worthless. The Egyptians believed Moses was better off dead; the Hebrews turned on him and rejected him as their leader countless times in the story of the Exodus. In the end, it was only God's opinion that mattered, as Moses was successful in both delivering the nation and establishing God's Law and the ordered worship of God.

You had a destiny long before others had an opinion about you.

The story of Joseph shows us how his brothers had a poor opinion about their young brother. They considered him utterly worthless and not much more than an aggravating kid brother. However, the opinions of Joseph's brothers didn't stop Joseph from becoming second-in-command in the nation of Egypt, as well as eventually even reigning over them.

An important key to killing your giant is to stop taking a poll of everyone's opinion before proceeding with what you believe your purpose to be. Your purpose will not be defined by a popular vote of what other people think about you. Your purpose will be defined by what God has destined for you, and then your willingness to both obey and pursue that purpose. In the story about the airport, I bet if we were to have asked the opinions of all the other travelers that were present that day, most would have thought that we would never make it to the Caribbean. Most would never think that we had a connection with a very powerful person who could, with one word, change our entire outcome. But we did.

Other people don't know what
you know and they may not know
who you know.

The Crucial Component

Remember, other people don't know what you know and they may not know who you know. Opinions are formed by assessing the information at hand and then formulating a position based on that knowledge. Even when others have all the same information you have, there is one ingredient that can turn all other information upside down. This one ingredient, this one word, is the most powerful word you need to know as you advance toward accomplishing your goals and killing your giant. This all-important word isn't luck; it is something profoundly more powerful and meaningful than that. It is the word faith.

In the story of the airport, there is one thing I left out. I didn't fail to mention it because it was unimportant. I waited to mention it because it was most important. As I was standing near the payphone waiting for the missionary to return my call, the young people on our trip had gathered together and begun to pray. These teenagers had spent several months in preparation for this trip, and they weren't going to allow it to go up in smoke over a simple policy change at the local airport. They wouldn't allow it to happen without a serious fight. As they prayed, they didn't approach this as uninformed teenagers. They approached it as people of faith who knew their God was capable of moving mountains. While others may have had various opinions about what the outcome would be, these kids refused to be deterred by that. They simply prayed.

Doubt will not have the final
answer in your life unless you
give it permission.

Regardless of the number of giants you may face or the size of the giants in your way, never underestimate the power of faith. When faith begins to rise up within you, it causes you to believe in such a way that the thoughts of others become completely inconsequential. It's not that you despise other people or discount their feelings, but true faith won't allow what others can't see to impact what you can see. These teenagers may have looked silly to onlookers as they were huddled up together, kneeling on the floor praying, but to the desperate, faith is far superior to what others may think.

Doubt will not have the final answer in your life unless you give it permission. In most difficult things we set out to accomplish, there will always be little voices of doubt that will arise as we continue on our journey. Every job that I have ever taken in my life has always been bigger than me at the outset. When I first became a youth pastor, I had limited experience, limited knowledge, and whole lot of uncertainty. As I began in the ministry, the chorus of negative voices became louder and louder until I made the decision to drown them out. I didn't do this by proving myself in some outlandish way or by openly declaring my own value. The way those voices were drowned out was by my own perseverance and by embracing the faith I had in knowing I was in God's will. Sometimes the way you defeat a giant is by simply outliving the opposition. There is power in saying, "I'm not going anywhere!"

Sometimes the way you defeat a giant is by simply outliving the opposition.

Later in life as a church planter and pastor, the voices of doubt were resurrected, and with greater intensity. I could not allow doubt to have the final answer. Yes, the jobs were bigger than me but I knew that God would give me the strength and wisdom I needed at the time I needed it. Perseverance refuses to quit, refuses to take shortcuts, and refuses to settle. Perseverance requires faith, as it isn't a one-time decision, but a lengthy process of defeating your giants on a daily basis. Nobody can simply flip a switch that makes them persevere. Often you have to remind yourself of your purpose and make a willful decision to refuse to settle for anything less.

Overlooked

When young David, the giant slayer, was originally noticed and then anointed by the prophet Samuel, those closest to him were full of doubts, but David managed to move beyond them. Remember how this all played out: David's father, Jesse, was told that the prophet Samuel was coming to make a sacrifice, and invited him and his sons to take part. When Samuel arrived, Jesse had invited seven of his sons and each of them passed before the prophet. As Samuel took note of each one, he noticed that something was wrong. The Lord had not chosen any of these men to become the next king of Israel.

> Thus Jesse made seven of his sons pass before Samuel. And Samuel said to Jesse, "The Lord has not chosen these." And Samuel said to Jesse, "Are all the young men here?" Then he said, "There remains yet the youngest, and there he is, keeping the sheep." And Samuel said to Jesse, "Send and bring him. For we will not sit down till he comes here." So he sent and brought him in. Now he was ruddy, with bright eyes, and good-looking. And the Lord said, "Arise, anoint him; for this is the one!" Then Samuel took the horn of

> oil and anointed him in the midst of his brothers;
> and the Spirit of the Lord came upon David from
> that day forward. So Samuel arose and went to
> Ramah (1 Samuel 16:10-13).

The message that was sent to the young shepherd boy was very clear: "You are not worthy to be considered among your brothers." A closer examination of this story will reveal that David was the youngest of the brothers. According to the traditional customs in that day, the eldest son was considered the greatest, even to the point of receiving a double portion of his father's inheritance when that time came. So the feeling of disdain was not only from the father, but also from David's brothers. As the youngest, he was bypassing each of his seven brothers in the familial pecking order. How did David ignore this obvious snub from his brothers and pursue his ultimate destiny anyway? We can find the answer to this in the passage we just read:

> Then Samuel took the horn of oil and anointed
> him in the midst of his brothers; and the Spirit of
> the Lord came upon David from that day forward
> (1 Samuel 16:13).

David's destiny was bigger than a childhood dream. It was more than a doting mother expecting the impossible for her son. David's destiny was sealed by the plans of the Lord Himself. To David, his calling was not a choice, it was a responsibility placed on his life. His sense of expectation about the future wasn't generated by a child pretending to have a certain profession; his expectation came from his faith in a God who believed in him.

When you begin to recognize that often the dreams placed inside your heart did not originate with you, but were placed inside of you by the Lord instead, it changes the value of your dream. When an objective is my own desire, I may work at it until I get tired of trying. However, when I realize that my objective is much more than my own desire, but an actual calling from God, now there is a weight of responsibility attached to it. David's brothers could easily disagree with his calling, and they were free to express that however they wanted. But for David it wasn't a matter of gaining the support of his siblings, it was now a matter obedience. Others won't understand your calling, but it's not theirs to understand, nor is it their responsibility to be faithful to that call. If I allow others to undermine my calling, it's not something I can blame on them. It's not their fault—it's solely mine!

> If I allow others to undermine my calling, it's not something I can blame on them. It's not their fault-it's solely mine!

As we read the story of David, one thing stands out about the way he carried himself during his season of preparation. He had to go back and continue as the youngest of the brothers. Only now he was despised and had to deal with the jealousy of his siblings. He went back to being a shepherd, just like he was before he was anointed by the prophet. However, during this awkward and difficult season, we see that David remained faithful. It's much easier to be faithful to your calling when everything lines up and people are cheering you on. It's a completely different thing when even those closest to you can't seem to support you—or worse yet, are jealous and want to see you fail.

We first see David's true potential as a man of great faith and a warrior king during the famous battle between him and Goliath. His interaction with his brothers shed some light on how much they despised him and how much they wanted him to fail. In this epic story of grace and faith, the stage is set for God to open the curtain and reveal His next king.

> Now the Philistines gathered their armies together to battle, and were gathered at Sochoh, which belongs to Judah; they encamped between Sochoh and Azekah, in Ephes Dammim. And Saul and the men of Israel were gathered together, and they encamped in the Valley of Elah, and drew up in battle array against the Philistines. The Philistines stood on a mountain on one side, and Israel stood on a mountain on the other side, with a valley between them (1 Samuel 17:1-3).

As we continue to read the story, it is painfully clear that there is no warrior among the Hebrews willing to fight the giant. The champion from Gath makes a daily ritual of taunting the armies of Israel, challenging both them and their God. David is sent by his father to deliver

kill the giant.

food to his brothers. Note that David isn't there to do battle. He is sent to bring takeout to his warrior brothers. Isn't it interesting that the warriors are afraid to fulfill their purpose, but the takeout guy ends up more than willing to do their job? One would think that in this environment infused with fear and terror, the men would be happy for anyone to stand up. At least there's a remote chance of victory when you have a volunteer. At this point, there was zero chance of victory as nobody was willing to fight. What we find, though, is quite the opposite.

> Then David spoke to the men who stood by him, saying, "What shall be done for the man who kills this Philistine and takes away the reproach from Israel? For who is this uncircumcised Philistine, that he should defy the armies of the living God?" And the people answered him in this manner, saying, "So shall it be done for the man who kills him." Now Eliab his oldest brother heard when he spoke to the men; and Eliab's anger was aroused against David, and he said, "Why did you come down here? And with whom have you left those few sheep in the wilderness? I know your pride and the insolence of your heart, for you have come down to see the battle" (1 Samuel 17:26-28).

Eliab doesn't speak as a concerned brother, fearful for the life of his younger sibling. No, he gushes out venomous criticism in his jealousy. Void of both concern and encouragement, Eliab takes a jab at David's shepherding vocation. Sometimes those you expect to help you are the ones who prove to be against you.

Chapter 8: The Final Answer

Again, don't expect others to shoulder the responsibility of your calling. David's response to his brother can serve as a template as to how we should respond to those who are critical of our efforts.

> And David said, "What have I done now? Is there not a cause?" Then he turned from him (1 Samuel 17:29-30a).

David didn't waste time defending himself or justifying his actions. The time you spend trying to convince others to believe in you is valuable time you could spend moving toward your purpose. Once David realized that Eliab was against him, he moved on and chose not to allow that to undermine his objective. David quickly answered and turned away from his brother to continue pursuing his purpose. David's response to his brother is a key to understanding why he could not be dissuaded. He says, "Is there not a cause?" David was forming his reason behind his purpose. As discussed in the last chapter, your *why* will push you even when opposition is strong against you.

The time you spend trying to convince others to believe in you is valuable time you could spend moving toward your purpose.

Seasons of Growth

One other thing about David's brothers that is worth noting is that you hear very little about any of them after this incident. David, of course, goes on to eventually become king and lead the nation to unprecedented victories. By the time of his death, Israel was sitting on a regional empire that was largely unchallenged. David had the ability to transition a peaceful kingdom to his son, Solomon, as a result of all the victories he had won. As you reflect on the treatment of David by his brothers, you realize that not only did their opinion not really matter, but they also faded into seclusion. The voices of opposition now will eventually become a nonissue later.

The voices of opposition now will eventually become a nonissue later.

The reason for this truth is that as you overcome opposition, you grow as a person. Things that use to bother me early in my ministry, no longer bother me now. I am no longer bound by people's opinions about how I should lead. It's not because everyone agrees with me now; it's just that by virtue of my own personal growth, I am confident in who I am and in what God has planned for me. When David was about to face off against Goliath, I'm sure the verbal attack by Eliab bothered him. I believe he longed for acceptance and wanted his brother to be proud of him, but in the end, those things could not be allowed to hinder his purpose. Goliath wasn't the only giant David killed that day; the giant of David's need for approval also died.

Chapter 8: The Final Answer

The real source of David's strength, however, was much more than his ability to move past disapproval and jealousy. David would now stand in front of a proven champion, a true warrior. David was not only dwarfed physically by Goliath, but he was dwarfed by comparison of experience. David's decision to fight the giant was not born on impulse. David had to reach down deep within himself to muster the strength and confidence to go through with his verbal commitment. He revealed his motivation as he stood before the giant as a lone warrior. Responding to Goliath's verbal assault and threats, David answered him:

> Then David said to the Philistine, "You come to me with a sword, with a spear, and with a javelin. But I come to you in the name of the Lord of hosts, the God of the armies of Israel, whom you have defied. This day the Lord will deliver you into my hand, and I will strike you and take your head from you. And this day I will give the carcasses of the camp of the Philistines to the birds of the air and the wild beasts of the earth, that all the earth may know that there is a God in Israel. Then all this assembly shall know that the Lord does not save with sword and spear; for the battle is the Lord's, and He will give you into our hands" (1 Samuel 17:45-47).

David's true source of strength was his faith in the Lord. The giant had man-made weaponry, but David knew his defense would come from God Himself. David's objective was not one of proving his own strength or

kill the giant.

worth, but proving the strength of God instead. David had an impressive track record of past victories. True, he had never fought against a giant, but he had killed lions and bears that had threatened his sheep. David could always come back to his testimony and remember the faithfulness of God.

When David hurled that rock and hit the giant in the forehead, striking a lethal blow, the Hebrews stood in astonishment. I believe everyone on both sides of that valley were in absolute shock: everyone, that is, except David. This was no surprise to David—a relief, yes, but not a surprise. It wasn't a surprise to him because the same faith that brought him *to* the battle was the faith that brought him *through* the battle. His faith was much deeper than killing a wild animal or a giant by the name of Goliath; his faith would prove to sustain him for his entire life and ministry as king of Israel.

You see, the final answer is not really about a *what*, it's about a *who*. The story of David and Goliath is not a story about two men. It's a story about a God who chose to use one man with faith to defeat another man who represented evil. David was known as the hero that day, but the true hero, of course, was the Lord. If David would have backed out and not faced the giant on the battlefield, God could have easily used someone else—in fact, anyone else. It wasn't David's skill with a sling that slayed the giant; it was David's unwavering faith that defeated what could have been a generational bondage over the people of Israel.

Chapter 8: The Final Answer

Life's challenges really come down to that repeated question from the old game show: "Is that your final answer?" You can take an answer from someone who lacks the authority to really close the deal, or you can choose to trust the Lord. Either way, know this: anything less than victory and the fulfillment of your purpose isn't final. At least, it doesn't have to be.

kill the giant.

8: The Final Answer
Action Points

Don't Stay Discouraged: When you find yourself a little discouraged—or even very discouraged—remember that *this feeling is always a choice*. Make the correct choice right now, to not allow that feeling to rob you of your plans and intent to succeed. The question isn't "Will you ever get discouraged?" That is a given, and you will. The better question is: "How long will you *stay* discouraged?" Nobody has the power to change your outlook and attitude but you. The understanding that you were created to succeed will help you move past periods of discouragement. You do not have to stay discouraged; and as an added bonus, every time you move past discouragement, it makes you a little stronger to be able to defeat your next bout.

> Blessed is the man who walks not in the counsel of the ungodly, nor stands in the path of sinners, nor sits in the seat of the scornful; but his delight is in the law of the Lord, and in His law he meditates day and night. He shall be like a tree planted by the rivers of water, that brings forth its fruit in its season, whose leaf also shall not wither; and whatever he does shall prosper (Psalm 1:1-3).

Never Accept *No* from Someone Who Doesn't Have the Authority to Say *Yes*: Do an honest analysis of your life and your current path. Are you on the path that will lead you to your ultimate accomplishment, or are you sidetracked somewhere along the way? If, after being honest about your path, you feel like you've gotten a little off course, I can almost guarantee there was a voice somewhere along the way that was instrumental in shifting your focus. Go back and revisit that moment, that conversation, that turning point, and find out how you went astray. Don't go back to fix the voice. Just go back to fix you! David could have listened to the many voices of dissent that he heard, but he knew down deep where his authority came from and that kept him locked onto his purpose.

Don't Get Bound to One-dimensional Thinking: You may not need to find a new solution to your problem. You may just need to adjust to the solution that is already in front of you. Have you exhausted all the possibilities with what you already have to work with? When a vehicle gets a new paint job, it doesn't make it run any better, but it sure feels like it. Before giving up and quitting on your dreams, carefully evaluate all the roads in front of you. You are probably much brighter than you realize, and you may have already considered a solution but didn't give it enough thought to make it viable. Don't just think bigger, think broader. More angles, more possibilities, more solutions: keep thinking it through. You'll get there.

Remember Who You Believe In: I want you to believe in yourself, but you can only do that if your faith is in the Lord. Nothing changes your perspective of God quite like worship. Take a minute right now and just praise Him. You'll see your perspective begin to shift. David was an impressive young shepherd boy, military leader, and king; his great success though came from the Lord. At the end of the day, we may be highly intellectual or very good at what we do, but never forget that without the Lord, we are nothing. However, with Him we can do all things!

Chapter 9: Shoo-In

When I was in college and even into my first year of marriage, I spent several years working for an electrical contractor. The world of construction was new to me, but I learned many life lessons and also some valuable practical how-tos that continue to help me to this day. The company I worked for was a large commercial outfit and they had their business down to a science in everything from the initial bidding process to the timeline for job completion. This company was one of the best in the business.

Every job started the same. The beginning days of work at a new jobsite required some underground work and then eventually moved to the point of laying out walls so piping could be stubbed up for receptacles and switches. This part of the job required a lot of labor support, not necessarily skilled labor, but just people who were willing to work. At this time, the construction industry was booming, and the company I worked for had more work than they could handle. As a result, they would hire most anyone who looked even remotely capable of some manual labor.

I quickly realized, however, that the hiring frenzy only lasted during the early stages of each job. Once the underground portion was complete, the work began to slow some as other trades became involved. It was no longer necessary to keep all the workers, as the workload now decreased. Remember, the company had this down to a science, and the all-important bottom line required that there would be layoffs.

The objective of new hires, at least for those who really wanted to keep a job, was to work as hard as possible in order to avoid having their name added to the list of the layoffs that would eventually come. It was not uncommon to see guys come in early for work and then work past quitting time. Each day we had a couple of fifteen-minute breaks, when some of the "eager-beavers" worked right through, just to showcase their great work ethic. This was all done in order to catch the eye of the job foreman, and hopefully avoid the dreaded layoff when the time came. Each person was working to prove themselves and hopefully stay on with permanent status. Without permanent status, each person was only a temporary worker and would be forced to jump from one company to the next as work began to slow. This, of course, was really nothing more than political posturing. Many of these guys weren't fantastic workers as much as they were fantastic actors. However, this did not stop them from trying to attain the all-important shoo-in status.

A *shoo-in* refers to someone or something who is sure to win. The term comes from early 1900s in American horse racing when dishonest jockeys intentionally lost so a specific horse could win, thereby assuring their crooked bets. Throughout your life, you have probably seen various examples of the shoo-in. Political elections in which the winning candidate wins by a landslide, or a sporting event where one team is obviously outmatched by the competition. Whatever the case, the shoo-in is marked by the predictability of certain victory. In my early days in the construction industry, this status was sought after to maintain employment and avoid the frustration of another job hunt.

A shoo-in refers to someone or something who is sure to win.

Status Revealed

Wouldn't it be something if we could maintain that status in life? Wouldn't you love the status of the shoo-in—of course without any deception or rigged politics? Wouldn't it be great to have some sort of innate advantage that just seemed to always propel you to the top? The benefit of the shoo-in is that competition becomes a nonissue. You don't have to be consumed with, or even be mildly concerned about, who's against you because, after all, you're a shoo-in!

Well, I've got some great news for you, probably some of the best news you'll hear all day. With God on your side, you are automatically a shoo-in! That's right! As a believer, you have the distinct advantage over anything that might hinder your success. If you have a hard time embracing this belief, here's just a few scriptures to help you realize your status.

> When I cry out to You, then my enemies will turn back; this I know, because God is for me (Psalm 56:9).

> The Lord is for me, so I will have no fear. What can mere people do to me? (Psalm 118:6 NLT).

> The Lord is for me among those who help me; therefore I shall see my desire on those who hate me (Psalm 118:7).

> For I know the thoughts that I think toward you, says the Lord, thoughts of peace and not of evil, to give you a future and a hope (Jeremiah 29:11).

> What then shall we say to these things? If God is for us, who can be against us? (Romans 8:31).

A prevalent theme in scripture is that God has a vested interest in our success. He doesn't stand by as a simple well-wisher, but He chooses to take part in our victory. David, one of the most famous giant-killers of all time, readily recognized that his successes were in large part due to the strength of God working in his life. David was brave, he was strong, he was ambitious and full of faith, but he was quick to credit his success to the Lord working on his behalf. So what does this looks like in our everyday life? We have to do everything we can do within our power to succeed, but we must understand that we have a distinct advantage, in that God is working for our success as well.

> We must understand that we
> have a distinct advantage, in
> that God is working for our
> success as well.

I am a strong believer in this principle, meaning that since I know that God is committed to my success, I carry something on me called *favor*. *Favor* is the word I'll use to describe the advantage that God gives the believer. If you've been serving the Lord for any length of time, you'll readily identify with moments in your life that you knew that Someone wasn't only looking out for you, He was actually contending for you. These moments are powerful reminders of the love of God, as well as proof that you are favored by the Lord. David was humbled by God's favor over his life. He wrote about it in Psalms.

> For You, O Lord, will bless the righteous; with favor You will surround him as with a shield (Psalm 5:12).

> For the Lord God is a sun and shield; the Lord bestows favor and honor; no good thing does he withhold from those whose walk is blameless (Psalm 84:11 NIV).

The favor of God, much like the grace of God, is not deserved or earned, but freely given. Just as we look at our own children with favor, God looks at His children with favor. As a parent, we will do things for our kids that we wouldn't do for anyone else. They are special to us. We had a part in their creation, and our DNA runs through their body. They are not perfect, but they are loved and eternally a part of who we are. As God's children, He knows that we are not perfect, yet He has a profound investment in us. He longs for us to succeed. He wants us to do well. He lives for the moments we win, and loves to see us full of joy.

He longs for us to succeed. He wants us to do well. He lives for the moments we win, and loves to see us full of joy.

I've often heard of, and seen demonstrated in my own life, the reality of God's favor extended toward me. One such example happened during one of our church's local outreaches. We had a group of well over 100 teenagers camping out at the church for an entire week. This camp was designed to both disciple kids and then give them real-life opportunities to reach out to others. On one particular day, we were scheduled to go to the local city park and play basketball and other games on the outdoor courts where the city was hosting a summer kids' camp. This required getting permits from the city, which was an extensive process, complete with liability releases, insurance riders, complete descriptions of the event, and much more. For religious and liability reasons, one of the contingencies of our permit was that we could not openly invite the kids participating in the city camp to be part of our games.

On the day of the event, there was a mild tropical storm hovering over our area. It was nothing serious, but certainly kept people from participating in anything outdoors. As our group of teenagers gathered in buses at the park, we realized that our plans were a complete washout—literally. We had purchased supplies, planned specific games, and our kids were really disappointed that we were not going to be able to proceed as planned. I placed a call to the director of the camp and let them know we would be leaving and returning to our facility to regroup. However (and this is where favor came in), the director practically begged me to come into the gymnasium where the kids' camp was being held and entertain all the rambunctious kids gathered there who were not able to go outside and burn off their energy.

This was something only God could have done. These were not any plans we had made. God was smiling down on us and created an opportunity for us. As we went into the gym, we were shocked to see over 150 small kids ready to be entertained. We quickly changed gears and did an entire kid's presentation of the gospel. I sent one of our teams back to the church to gather some supplies and we did it big! We had Christian rappers, dancers, puppets, skits, and more. At the end of the presentation, we gave an opportunity for kids to accept Jesus into their hearts—and the majority of the room responded and prayed with us that rainy day!

Favor cannot be planned, accounted for, or even explained; but as a believer in Christ, know that you have it. What started as a simple basketball game with a small number of kids, evolved into a rained-out event. Then favor stepped in and changed everything. There is no way in the world the city would have permitted us to do what we did, but God's favor put all the pieces into place. This event was incredibly successful and continues to be a legendary story around our campus to this day.

> If you aren't dead, then there is
> still hope!

When you look at the giant that is opposing you, you may feel outmatched, outnumbered, or outclassed. However, when you remember that God's favor is on your life, it gives you an air of confidence that says, "I may be outmatched, but I'm not defeated yet." If you aren't dead, then there is still hope! You've probably heard this old saying many times, but I still love it, "It's not over until God says it's over." Don't count yourself out too soon, and don't let others do that either. If there's still breath in you, then there's still life in you!

The Right Question

When it comes to defeating the giants in our lives, we often ask the wrong questions. We ask things like: "How can I possibly win?" or "What am I supposed to do?" or even "How could things get any worse?" These are not the right questions because these questions already assume defeat. The kind of reasoning that inspires a question like these is just a small step away from giving up altogether.

Years ago I used to help coach my young sons when they were playing city league football. Many of the kids who played for us came from homes that weren't supportive of them. In fact, much of the coaching consisted of speaking with disgruntled parents on the sidelines. We constantly dealt with parents yelling insults at their kids; instead of building them up, they consistently tore them down. I realized that these kids were in need of a truly positive role model, someone who would speak encouraging words to them, even when they made mistakes. I decided that God had put me there for that specific reason—so I could exemplify what they had never really experienced before.

It was often hard to encourage these kids when they began to lose in a game (which was often), as they tended to latch on to the negative and morale deteriorated quickly from there. In one game, we were getting beaten pretty severely. At halftime, these guys were all but finished. Their comments were: "We always lose," and "There's no way we can catch up now," and "Let's just forfeit." The head football coach of our team responded rather harshly to their "quitter" attitude. He lectured them for a good ten minutes on what sportsmanship was all about and how they needed to suck it up and play harder.

The custom in these events involves the assistant coaches each taking a turn and trying to share some kind of insight that might resonate with the kids. When it was my turn, I began to share with the boys about all the time they had spent in practice and how hard they had worked up until this point. I reminded them of how much their parents had invested in them and how proud of them they were. Then I told them they had to get their minds off how bad they were losing and begin to focus on playing to the best of their abilities. I reminded them of the statements they made when we started halftime, all the statements about impossibility and how pointless it was to continue. I asked them this simple question: "With an attitude that says we've already lost, do you think you could possibly win?" They all answered with a resounding, "No, sir!" I asked, "How do we fix that?" Silence ensued for a few seconds—which seemed like an eternity as I was afraid I was losing them—and then one of the boys chimed in, "We have to believe we can win." Bingo, now we're getting somewhere!

Some of the boys immediately added the word "but"; however, I quickly stopped them before they could complete their sentences. I said, "No buts. You have to believe you can win. Period." If you have already lost in your mind, it's just a matter of two more quarters and you'll lose on the field. The wrong question here is: "How can we possibly win?" while the right question is, "What do we need to do in order to win?" Thankfully some of the other coaches picked up on what I was trying to do. They could see that the boys were beginning to rethink their attitudes. The coaches all began to share some tweaks and adjustments on both sides of the ball and the morale of the team began to shift. As I was the only coach who was also a pastor, the head coach asked me to pray for the team before playing the second half just to seal the deal. I prayed a prayer about how proud we were and how proud God was of these boys. I said we believed in them, regardless of the results, and we knew they could win.

It would make a great story to tell you that our boys came back and won the game with a resounding victory, but that didn't happen. However, those boys played like I had never seen them play before. They did close much of the losing gap, and even though it was not a victory, it was definitely a respectable loss. I still believe that had their attitudes been right from the start, the final score would have been much different. At the end of the game I bragged on those kids and told them how proud I was. I told them that even though the scoreboard was lopsided, they played like absolute champions. As I remember it, our season shifted after that game. No, we weren't county champs by any stretch of the imagination, but we certainly produced a quality group of young boys who loved the game of football.

> When we speak words of defeat,
> we are already in the planning
> stages of walking in that defeat.

When we speak words of defeat, we are already in the planning stages of walking in that defeat. I have witnessed patients in the hospital whose health began to deteriorate dramatically as soon as they heard a negative prognosis over their condition. An attitude of defeat is a battle all to itself; it sidelines focus, faith, and energy to fight the real battle at hand. When we understand that we have God's favor on our lives and that we are automatic shoo-ins for victory, we should be asking different questions.

Instead of wondering if we could possibly win, we should be thinking, *How can I possibly fail?* Faith is the largest part of this mindset, but we also have to understand that we are in this thing for the long haul. There are times when we get knocked down, but that doesn't mean we have to stay down. Most teams who win championships in their sport also suffer quite a bit of defeat along the way. Bad play calls, injuries, coaching problems, heartbreaking losses, and more are a part of sustaining a legacy-building team.

For a true giant-killer, loss is never an option.

I often tell people, "You are either *in* a battle or you are in preparation *for* a battle." You won't face only one giant in your lifetime. You will probably face numerous giants throughout the years. A winner's attitude looks back at past achievements and thinks, *I believe we can do even more.* A winner's attitude looks back at past losses, thinking, *We have something to learn from that, and it has made us even stronger.* For a true giant-killer, loss is never an option. Killing your giant is rarely a short-

Chapter 9: Shoo-In

term commitment; in fact, it is usually harder than you thought it would be, more strenuous than you dreamed it could be, and more painful than you ever imagined. There's a reason a giant got to be a giant: nobody ever killed it.

But you have favor and you are a shoo-in for success. It may take you some time to get there, but you can and will win. The shoo-in knows that victory isn't something that's simply possible, it's something that is *probable*. As a giant-killer, you will have to think differently than other people. As I mentioned in chapter 5, many people had their opportunity to kill the giants, but nobody did until David came along. Why was that? Where others saw danger and impossibility, David saw victory and reward. For David, it wasn't just positive thinking techniques or a desire to prove his worth as a warrior; he truly believed that God would use him to do what nobody else could do.

A true giant-killer has to
develop a mindset that runs
more like a machine than a
thermometer.

A true giant-killer has to develop a mindset that runs more like a machine than a thermometer. The thermometer has no choice but to respond to its environment: when the temperature goes down, the mercury drops, and when the temperature goes up, the mercury rises. That kind of mentality works well when things in your life are going smoothly, but when you face your giant, it's a completely different story. A machine, on the other hand, operates from the standpoint of original design. A vacuum will vacuum whether it's hot or cold. A car will drive and operate in all kinds of weather. A telephone doesn't care about its placement, environment, cleanliness, or anything else for that matter. It is a machine and designed to work, regardless of its surroundings.

Giant-killers have to function from the perspective of original design. Our minds have been impacted by a world full of negativity, unbelief, and doubt, so we have to allow our minds to be renewed by a different way of thinking. Our Creator didn't design us to be failures. He designed us to withstand and overcome the challenges that come our way. Romans gives us a reminder about the power of the mind.

> And do not be conformed to this world, but be transformed by the renewing of your mind, that you may prove what is that good and acceptable and perfect will of God (Romans 12:2).

The world pushes for conformity, the same kind of conformity that lacks the ability to believe you can kill your giant. But this conformity is defeated; it is defeated by a mind that is transformed by renewal. When something is renewed, it starts all over—like a complete system reboot. If you have any automatically-renewed annual subscriptions, you've seen this happen firsthand. Once your year is up, the subscription automatically starts over for an additional year. The past year is no longer relevant. The new year is all that counts, and you

Chapter 9: Shoo-In

better believe that you are being billed accordingly. The mind that is renewed is now thinking on a different plane than it used to think. The old way of thinking is no longer relevant; the renewed subscription has taken over, and Jesus has paid the bill!

In Romans 12:2 above, the writer says, "that you may prove what is that good and acceptable and perfect will of God." The perfect will of God is not proven by a mind full of doubt and defeatist thinking, it is proven by conforming to the Word of God. A mind shaped by the world will reek of doubt and negativity, but a mind that has been transformed by God's Word will be full of faith and power. God doesn't fight against you. He fights for you. We have to know that. How is it that we have favor? How is it that we are shoo-ins? We have an advantage because while others may be fighting against us, God is fighting *for* us.

> A mind shaped by the world will reek of doubt and negativity, but a mind that has been transformed by God's Word will be full of faith and power.

If you find yourself experiencing discouragement and drowning in negativity, it's time to examine your mind. Begin to pray and ask the Lord to help you think differently and stop being driven by your emotions instead of faith. David the giant-killer had to do this; in fact, he recorded his prayer to the Lord.

kill the giant.

> Search me, O God, and know my heart; try me, and know my anxieties; and see if there is any wicked way in me, and lead me in the way everlasting (Psalm 139:23-24).

Think from a Position of Success

Being positive and maintaining an attitude of faith is not about being self-reliant. In fact, it's quite the opposite. When I find myself relying too heavily on my own abilities, I make mistakes—big mistakes. A lasting attitude of faith is developed through surrender. Giant-killers are bold and strong, but they realize their strength comes from the Lord. We aren't shoo-ins because we are deserving, we are shoo-ins because of His grace. In the story of David and Goliath, one combatant had faith in himself, while the other had his faith in the Lord. Faith in God will always win over faith in one's self.

A lasting attitude of faith is developed through surrender.

We have to begin to think from a position of success rather than failure. Too often our thoughts are, *Why should I be successful?* This must be changed to: *Why shouldn't I be successful?* You are born to be a giant-killing machine; you are born to be successful; you are born to win; you already have the advantage and you are a shoo-in! Thinking from a position of success already assumes victory rather than defeat. Defeat gives up before the battle even starts; victorious thinking already knows the end result and braces for the upcoming challenges.

In many animal herds, there is an alpha male. This one animal is the undisputed leader and has the responsibility to protect the whole herd. Whether we are talking about wolves, zebras, or lions, the herd seldom makes decisions without the leadership of the alpha male. This particular animal is usually the strongest, fastest, and most competent for the job. The very ability to sustain the life of the herd depends upon the success of this one animal. At first glance, an alpha male might appear arrogant or conceited, but there is a difference between cockiness and self-confidence.

Thinking from a position of
success already assumes victory
rather than defeat.

An alpha male doesn't have the luxury of lounging around and being overly concerned with the thoughts of the others in the herd. The feelings of others aren't his focal point. Survival is. This animal knows his responsibility, and will not only readily defend himself, but will also quickly defend the safety and security of the herd he's been charged to protect. The self-confidence he displays is not an indication of pride or being consumed with himself, but rather a healthy understanding of his role in the life of the herd. If the alpha male stopped to question himself on every decision or even hesitate to see what the others thought, this could cost valuable time and allow a predator to injure or even destroy the herd.

If an alpha male thinks from a position of defeat, it means he has already surrendered to whatever is threatening the herd. He absolutely cannot allow himself to think on a plane that even remotely concedes defeat; this would not only be costly, but would most likely end in death. Many times when we are faced with a problem, we immediately begin to consider all the possibilities of defeat. If I don't land a job pretty soon, then I'll be forced to give up my house. If my son or daughter doesn't start making better decisions, they are going to end up in jail. Why do we immediately allow our thinking to assume defeat? Similar to an alpha male, our way of thinking is more than a simple attitude adjustment. Our survival depends on it. There are quite a few lessons we can learn from an alpha male in terms of how we approach defeating the things that are bigger than us.

An alpha male doesn't think about the consequences of failure. Instead, he devotes his energy to creating the path to victory. Think about a dominant alpha male in a crisis situation; as danger approaches, he has to go on the offensive. If he assumed a posture of cowering or hiding, it would leave the rest of the herd vulnerable to danger. The alpha knows that survival depends on quick, decisive action that displays a show of force and the refusal to be intimidated by anyone or anything. I am certainly not saying that anytime we are threatened we should go on the attack, but our thinking needs to be generated from the mindset of victory. An alpha male has fought for his position; it was not handed to him. What you have accomplished in life thus far has been by the grace of God coupled with your hard work. You cannot allow that to be taken from you without a fight; remember you are a shoo-in.

In the biblical story of David standing on the battlefield against the giant from Gath, he stood with a lot of poise and confidence. He absolutely trusted in the Lord, but let's not discount the fact that that took a lot of guts! It's easy for us to read that old story and quickly discount how David must have felt on that day, standing in the valley in front of this massive, experienced warrior. I have no doubt that his stomach was in knots, his palms were sweaty, and his mouth was dry. David was full of faith, but let's not forget that he was a human being too. Anyone in that position would have some anxiety. David didn't voice his concern over what would happen if he lost. He didn't allow his mind to ponder what a loss would look or feel like; he only considered victory. David didn't write a note home to his parents, telling them of his final wishes if he were to die. He could not afford to think from a position of loss. His conversation that day wasn't one of possible defeat, but of certain victory. When David plead his case to King Saul, asking for permission to represent Israel in battle against the giant, his confidence was obvious.

> But David said to Saul, "Your servant used to keep his father's sheep, and when a lion or a

bear came and took a lamb out of the flock, I went out after it and struck it, and delivered the lamb from its mouth; and when it arose against me, I caught it by its beard, and struck and killed it. Your servant has killed both lion and bear; and this uncircumcised Philistine will be like one of them, seeing he has defied the armies of the living God." Moreover David said, "The Lord, who delivered me from the paw of the lion and from the paw of the bear, He will deliver me from the hand of this Philistine" (1 Samuel 17:34-37).

Notice David never said, "I might win," or "Maybe the Lord will deliver him into my hand." David's wording did not allow for questioning. He spoke with confidence because he *was confident,* and his perspective was positioned securely on that confidence he had in the Lord. David's faith in God had brought him to this point. He had seen God's hand on his life to defeat both lions and bears. It would have been easy to say, "Yeah, but, David, this giant is no lion or bear; he is a champion!" But that's just it: to David the type of obstacle wasn't the issue. To David, it was all the same. If God helped him defeat those enemies, then God would help him defeat this enemy. How could he say that? David knew that the grace of God on his life made him a shoo-on.

9: Shoo-in
Action Points

Daily Affirmation: Remind yourself daily that God is fighting for you and that He is on your side. If you are going through a particularly hard season, you may want to remind yourself of this over and over throughout the day. The Scriptures outlined in this chapter are evidence of God's attitude towards you. He believes in you and is committed to your success. Say things like this: "I know that God is for me," "I know that God believes in me," "I am sure that I will succeed," and "I have no doubt that I will conquer this." These things may seem trivial, but sometimes you have to keep speaking these ideas to yourself until they begin to register within the reservoir of your own faith. David wasn't born as a man of great faith. He *became* a man of great faith as he saw God's hand working in his life over and over.

Assume Victory, Not Defeat: Others may have made you feel like you aren't good enough to win. Some may have discounted your effectiveness, your viability, or your potential; somebody has to win, so why not you and why not now? You can't wait until you win to start thinking like a winner. You have to think like a winner before you'll ever become a winner. Nobody wins a championship by surprise. It takes a lot of work and a lot of proper attitude and mindset.

Flip the Switch: Not only can you not entertain negative or defeatist thoughts yourself, but sometimes you have to forcibly remove yourself from those who do. It may appear rude or seem unfriendly, but your faith has to remain strong at all costs. As we discussed in Chapter 8, David didn't spend much time with his brother Eliab. He quickly dismissed both his conversation and his presence. David flipped the switch on negativity, lack of faith, and unbelief in the power of God. Give yourself permission right now to *flip the switch.*

Rise Higher: You are a shoo-in, not because you are dripping with natural talent or ability, but because you are a child of God, and He fights your battles for you. When a situation arises, an enemy approaches, or difficulty emerges, know immediately that you have already won. The question isn't whether or not you can win, it is how will your victory manifest itself? I know my giant is already in the process of dying. I just have to figure out how to see that come to completion. As an eagle flies, he continues to gain altitude until he reaches a soaring height. It's not until he rises that he soars high above any predators, obstacles, or hindrances. He could stay on the ground, but he chooses to rise higher. I encourage you today to do the same. Get up above your challenges and rise higher!

Chapter 10: Kill Your Giant!

The Christmas season really is the most wonderful time of the year. Recently, my wife and I spent some time away in a small town just before the holidays got into full swing. The small Mom-and-Pop shops down the local roads were hanging decorations on the fronts of their stores as well as putting up Christmas trees, complete with lights and festive music inside. Along the public roads, city workers were busy up in their bucket trucks, hanging pennant-style decorations from the tall light poles. The sights and sounds of the Christmas season are joyous and often bring back childhood memories of special gifts and time spent with friends and family.

One of the common holiday activities for most families is placing gifts around the family Christmas tree. When our kids were young (and even to this day), they would dig through the presents and see how many and how big their presents were. As they looked, you would inevitably hear these exciting words: "Here's mine!" or "Here's another one that's mine!" Of course, this would be followed by close inspections. Gifts were held up in the air and shaken to guess their contents. This investigation also included a comparison between the siblings of who may have gotten the most or whose gifts were the best. As a side note, my wife has always been very meticulous about making certain all the children get the exact same number of gifts under the tree. However, this would never thwart the pre-Christmas snooping under the old Christmas tree.

The kids knew they were handling their own gift because their name was written on a tag on the outside. The tag designated that this particular gift had been purchased, wrapped, and placed under the tree just for them. If one of my three precious angels began to touch or shake another sibling's gift, there was an immediate response of, "Hey, that's mine!" The name on the outside of the gift implied that person's ownership. Could you imagine what a free-for-all would ensue if you had a Christmas tree loaded with gifts but without name tags? There would be fussing and fighting; boys would be opening baby dolls, and girls opening cowboy outfits and who knows what else. It would create mass confusion and hysteria and probably spoil the fun of the whole day.

The name tag creates a designation that shows love for the person receiving the gift. It is also administrative in that it stops the confusion of mistaken identity. Without the name tag, the gift has no owner and becomes useless as a blessing or source of joy for the intended recipient. But with a name tag, there is a sense of confidence that this gift was intended for a specific person and was carefully chosen to show the love of the giver.

Chapter 10: Kill Your Giant!

In our lives, there are many things that we have to face as individuals. Specific things that nobody sees the same way we do; after all, we're the ones in the situation. Many of these things are great and we celebrate them: marrying our spouse, the birth of children, the celebration of special days, and many other joyous moments. However, many of the things we face aren't so celebratory: job loss, sickness, or the death of people who are close to us. Regardless, these are all moments we have to experience and handle. The fun moments are great, but there is no free pass in life that can guarantee we will never have hardship, heartache, or pain. The good and the bad both have one thing in common: the name tag that bears our name. Like the gift under the Christmas tree, the moments of our lives are identified as our moments; we can't shift ownership to others to face what has been given to us. Most of us will have to handle crisis, difficulty, and painful moments (or even painful seasons) in our lives.

There is no free pass in
life that can guarantee we
will never have hardship,
heartache, or pain.

It's Not All Fun and Games

Like you, I wish all of my moments could be joyous, happy celebrations that mark the high points in life, but the truth is we seldom grow from the happy, high-water

kill the giant.

marks of our lives. Like a seed buried in the ground, our greatest growth emerges in the darkness of defeat. When we're hurting, it forces us to dig into the intellectual, spiritual, and emotional places much deeper than we would like to. These places of depth provide a fertile reservoir of sustaining strength to help us face not only the current challenge, but those yet to come.

> Like a seed buried in the ground,
> our greatest growth emerges in
> the darkness of defeat.

Have you ever looked at someone and thought, *Wow, they are such a strong person. I don't know how they can possibly handle that situation?* I can just about guarantee that, at the time of your observation, they didn't feel very strong. In fact, they most likely felt like they were right at their breaking point. Yet, pain and crisis has a way of highlighting our own strength. You learn things about yourself in those moments—things you never really knew before. Were it not for pain, you would have no idea what you were capable of overcoming.

In *The Left-Handed Warrior*, I wrote extensively about the miracle in our own lives in my wife's battle with breast cancer. Those days were a challenge, but really showed us some things about ourselves. I knew my wife was a strong woman and able to endure pain. After all, I was there as she gave birth to our three kids, but watching her walk through that season of uncertainty revealed her true inner strength. The challenges of family,

234

marriage, and ministry didn't take a break just because we were suffering. They all continued at warp speed. Now, several years on the other side of that shocking news and the ensuing treatment, we understand how defeating that giant has made us even stronger. Sometimes your curse will become your catalyst!

Sometimes your curse will become
your catalyst!

A Lesson from the Giants

As the children of Israel moved into their promised land, it was everything that God had said it would be, but the people soon realized that there were giants in the land. When you read the story of the initial fact-finding team, otherwise known as spies, you get a real sense of how quickly the visions of sunshine and rainbows were quickly crushed by reality.

> Now they departed and came back to Moses and Aaron and all the congregation of the children of Israel in the Wilderness of Paran, at Kadesh; they brought back word to them and to all the congregation, and showed them the fruit of the land. Then they told him, and said: "We went to the land where you sent us. It truly flows with milk and honey, and this is its fruit. Nevertheless the people who dwell in the land are strong; the cities are fortified and very large; moreover we saw the descendants of Anak there (Numbers 13:26-28).

kill the giant.

Everything that God had promised was accurate, but He apparently failed to mention the fact that there were giants in the land. Why would God have left out this seemingly-very-important tidbit of information? Was God playing a cruel trick? Or was He the proctor in an exam that would define the faith of these people, as well as the generations to come? Nothing God had promised the people was inaccurate; everything He said was absolutely true. The problem here was not misinformation; the problem was that they were getting distracted by details that didn't matter. Much like the people of Israel, we can easily lose our focus by getting distracted by irrelevant information.

Much like the people of Israel, we can easily lose our focus by getting distracted by irrelevant information.

The things we focus on intently have a tendency to grow larger. Think about it for a minute. If you are driven to manage money and curtail spending, closely watching the bottom line, and exerting energy to make sure it stays healthy, most likely the bottom line will grow bigger. If you pay no attention to the bottom line and act willy-nilly with your budget, the chances of growing wealth are severely minimized. If you exert energy and focus on all the negative issues in your life, you can easily become distracted with problems instead of solutions.

Chapter 10: Kill Your Giant!

Instead of finding answers to problems, you simply see bigger problems.

The Israelites saw problems, and these problems took the form of the giant descendants of Anak. Undeniably, these giants were a problem for the natural man, but God had given them a promise over the land they were to possess. Instead of being consumed with their promise, they became consumed with their problem. Guess what? Their problem became bigger and bigger. The giants weren't growing any bigger; they weren't multiplying any faster, but you sure wouldn't have known that by the terror amongst those reporting back to the people. What started out as a concern about giants erupted into a full-blown protest—and almost became a brawl among the people!

> So all the congregation lifted up their voices and cried, and the people wept that night. And all the children of Israel complained against Moses and Aaron, and the whole congregation said to them, "If only we had died in the land of Egypt! Or if only we had died in this wilderness! Why has the Lord brought us to this land to fall by the sword, that our wives and children should become victims? Would it not be better for us to return to Egypt?" So they said to one another, "Let us select a leader and return to Egypt" (Numbers 14:1-4).

Do you see what is happening here? The misguided focus on the wrong information grew bigger, thus undermining their original God-ordained purpose. Focus isn't just a factor in success; focus is everything! When you lose focus on the right thing, you will get sidelined by almost anything. God didn't formulate a plan for the people of Israel to possess land and forget about the existence of the giants. To kill the giants in your life, focus is key; but proper focus requires faith that God will take care of you.

> When you lose focus on the right thing, you will get sidelined by almost anything.

God knew all the details about the impending obstacles the people would face as they entered the land of Canaan. There was absolutely nothing that would surprise the Lord. He knew there would be some challenges, but He also knew He was capable of handling every situation ahead of them. The fact that they didn't know there were giants in the land was no indicator of God's lack of planning. It just showed that God refused to allow insignificant things to undermine His purpose.

God didn't tell them the parts of the story that didn't matter. Giants were not an issue for the Lord, He had no fear or doubt about the future for His chosen people. You've probably thought these things many times: *I didn't realize it was going to be like this!* or *I didn't know it was going to be this hard.* There's a reason why we don't get all the information up front before launching into new territories. If we knew everything that was going to happen in our future, we'd probably pull our head back into its shell like a turtle, and chicken out on our future adventures.

Another key point is that God could have removed the giants before the people entered, but He chose to leave them there. God could have stricken the giants with disease. He could have raised up another foreign army to hunt them, or He could have simply made them vanish, but He didn't. The giants weren't there to be a problem for the people of Israel. They were there to deepen their trust in God. The people of Israel needed to kill the giants to firmly establish themselves in their faith. They needed to learn for themselves that God would be faithful to keep them and establish them as a nation. Had someone else killed those giants, these people would have never had their faith tested. God knew their faith needed to grow so they could experience His love for them on a deeper and more personal level.

Don't get distracted by waiting for someone else to do what you have been destined to do.

The giants in the land of Canaan weren't just giants. They were specifically Israel's giants. They were born for the purpose of being killed by God's people to show His power and might. Listen, the giant you are facing in your life right now isn't just any giant. *It's your giant.* This giant, which may have taken a number of forms, like doubt, fear, insecurity, poverty, or many others, is not someone else's giant to kill. *It's your giant to kill.*

kill the giant.

You don't need someone else to kill this giant for you. In fact, that would be the worst thing that could happen to you. If someone else killed your giant, you'd lose the opportunity for an incredible increase in your own personal faith.

Don't get distracted by waiting for someone else to do what you have been destined to do. If God didn't know you could overcome your current obstacle, He would never have allowed it in the first place. God's interest is never in defeating you; His interest is in empowering you to do what you never thought possible. Remember, we serve a God who does not operate in the realm of impossibility. Anything is possible with God! Stop waiting for your giant to die of old age. It has your name on it because God wants you to experience that victory.

Catastrophe or Catalyst?

In those moments when we face our biggest giants, it is easy for us to be so consumed by fear that we miss the growth component. I'm sure you've heard the saying, "Bigger levels mean bigger devils." I'll tell you from experience, that's a true statement! The issues I face today are of a much greater magnitude than the issues I used to face years ago. As a believer who has worked to be faithful to God, there's much more at stake now than in previous years. I now have grown children and grandchildren, a larger ministry reach, and much more responsibility. The Enemy knows that the little devils are no longer effective against me and my family; that's why

Chapter 10: Kill Your Giant!

he sends stronger resistance to attack the work of our hands. But there is a growth component for us: every time we succeed against a giant obstacle, we grow to be able to face even bigger ones.

Sometimes our worst catastrophe can be our greatest catalyst! How many times have you heard of people who went through some great tragedy, yet overcame their tragedy successfully and developed it later into a platform to help others? Past drug addicts and alcoholics often make the best counselors and coaches for present addicts. Someone who has struggled with deep financial crisis and bankruptcy can often find a future in coaching others on how to conquer their money issues. Couples who have been through the fire of intense marital strife and walked through that pain successfully usually have a great message for other couples who are now struggling. A list of successful overcomers can include those who have defeated medical challenges, grief over loss, and many other real-life adversities. Without the challenge, there would never be the experience of total victory.

Sometimes our worst catastrophe can be our greatest catalyst!

Even the landscape of the earth teaches us this important lesson. Between every mountain lies a valley. You often have to walk through the pain of the valley in order to appreciate the view from the top of the mountain. Know this though: Time spent in the valley is never wasted, as it is valuable in building your faith and resolve. Begin to view the valley as a ramping-up season to give you the momentum necessary to get to the top of your next mountain. Every low point indicates that there's another high point on the way. I have noticed that a deeper valley means a higher mountain is yet to come! Be encouraged today. Valleys can't continue forever; you're well on your way to the next victory.

You often have to walk through the pain of the valley in order to appreciate the view from the top of the mountain.

The valley is where we grow. It's where we breathe hard and often question every step, but the mountaintop is where we inhale and enjoy the blessing of peace. Jesus was careful to convey this truth to His followers. He didn't shelter them from potential danger, pain, or difficult circumstances. Jesus led His disciples to funeral processions to see the pain of grieving up close. He took them to places in which people were experiencing hunger and the pain of debilitating disease. However, He was also careful to not just allow them to see other people's challenges; He wanted His followers to walk through some challenges of their own.

One evening Jesus was speaking to a crowd that had gathered to hear Him preach. To the disciples, this looked like any other night, but they were in for a rude awakening. Jesus was going to use an upcoming storm as a teachable moment to build their faith. He and His followers jumped in a boat to presumably make a quick trip to the other side, when all of a sudden, the simple plan came to a screeching halt.

> On the same day, when evening had come, He said to them, "Let us cross over to the other side." Now when they had left the multitude, they took Him along in the boat as He was. And other little boats were also with Him. And a great windstorm arose, and the waves beat into the boat, so that it was already filling. But He was in the stern, asleep on a pillow. And they awoke Him and said to Him, "Teacher, do You not care that we are perishing?" Then He arose and rebuked the wind, and said to the sea, "Peace, be still!" And the wind ceased and there was a great calm. But He said to them, "Why are you so fearful? How is it that you have no faith?" And they feared exceedingly, and said to one another, "Who can this be, that even the wind and the sea obey Him!" (Mark 4:35-41).

You will often be required to face your giant without any warning at all.

The wording in the second verse has always jumped out to me. It reads: "they took Him…as He was" which sounds a little odd. These words are referring to what looked like an impulsive, even hasty, decision. "As He was" meant without any preparation or any notice. Jesus didn't take an extra change of clothes, pack additional food, or even notify the crowds about where He was headed. "As He was" meant just that: "Right now, in this condition, let's go." It's important to realize that you will often be required to face your giant without any warning at all. This isn't because God doesn't know it is coming; it is because reliance upon God is often taught best in the moment of crisis.

The disciples thought this would be another quick trip across the Sea of Galilee, but while they were enjoying a relaxing boat ride, they soon realized a storm was brewing just offshore. It's interesting how trusting the disciples were when they were experiencing calm waters. Nobody questioned Jesus about the logic of getting into a boat at night without really knowing the conditions in the middle of the dark waters. However, when things got a little rocky, they were quick to blame it on Him. "Teacher, do you not care that we are perishing?" How quickly their trust eroded into panic.

> Jesus in the boat during the
> calm is the same Jesus in the
> boat during the storm.

The giants who oppose us will not only show up without advance warning, but they will challenge our faith to its very core. We can be going along life's road without a care in the world, when suddenly things change. We always have to remember that the Jesus in the boat during the calm is the same Jesus in the boat during the storm. This story has always made me laugh, not at the panic of the disciples, but at the fact that Jesus was found sleeping during the storm. Not only was He asleep, but as you read carefully you'll see, He was asleep on a pillow. This means He didn't just nod off and fall asleep during the journey. Sleeping had been part of His plan!

The disciples were in full crisis mode, complete with screaming, scurrying, and sliding about on the wet deck. It was a boat full of drama, yet Jesus was sleeping soundly without a care in the world. When the reality of the sudden storm sunk in, to their credit, the disciples quickly turned to Jesus. Much to their shock, Jesus wasn't participating in their dramatic confusion, He was at perfect peace. Jesus already knew what they would soon learn: He was the Master of the storm.

If we never had to battle our giants, we would miss the opportunities to trust God when it counted most.

Jesus could have calmed the storm before the boat ever launched. The disciples would not have even known that storm existed. But there was purpose in this travel— and it was much bigger than Jesus showing His power over the weather. Jesus was teaching the disciples that trust had to go deeper than enjoying calm waters; trust was proven in the midst of turbulent crisis. If we never had to battle our giants, we would miss the opportunities to trust God when it counted most.

kill the giant.

These men had faith in Jesus before this story unfolded, but can you imagine how much more confidence they had in Him afterward? In fact, we get a little glimpse of their response at the end of the passage. "And they feared exceedingly, and said to one another, 'Who can this be, that even the wind and the sea obey Him!'" These guys got more than a small faith boost from this experience. They were launched into a completely different realm of faith altogether. You would never be able to convince these guys that God had limitations. Why? They had a dead giant, in the form of a storm, to show what God could do. Each giant you conquer is another testimony in the building blocks of your faith. These men believed because they had seen firsthand what Jesus was capable of. It's a good thing their faith was now stronger because Jesus was about to bring them along to fight yet another giant. Fresh off one victory, the next spiritual battle would be even more intense.

Then they came to the other side of the sea, to the country of the Gadarenes. And when He had come out of the boat, immediately there met Him out of the tombs a man with an unclean spirit, who had his dwelling among the tombs; and no one could bind him, not even with chains, because he had often been bound with shackles and chains. And the chains had been pulled apart by him, and the shackles broken in pieces; neither could anyone tame him. And always, night and day, he was in the mountains and in the tombs, crying out and cutting himself with stones. When he saw Jesus from afar, he ran and worshiped Him. And he cried out with a loud voice and said, "What have I

to do with You, Jesus, Son of the Most High God?
I implore You by God that You do not torment me."
For He said to him, "Come out of the man, unclean
spirit!" Then He asked him, "What is your name?"
And he answered, saying, "My name is Legion;
for we are many" (Mark 5:1-9).

Jesus brought these men successfully through a storm
to build their faith, only to put them in another situation
that would require even more faith. Remember, each
giant you face is preparation for the next giant you will
face. As they stepped out of the boat and onto the shore,
the disciples had just breathed a sigh of relief to be on
solid ground again when they were suddenly met by a
wild demoniac who could not be physically restrained.
These men, though gazing with eyes as big as dinner
plates at this new development, dared not question the
God they had seen conquer the storm. For them, this
giant was intimidating and unpredictable, but their latest
catastrophe had been a catalyst to help them believe that
Jesus could do anything. It was the plan of God all along
to raise up the giants so faith could defeat them.

Each giant you face is
preparation for the next giant
you will face.

Your Time Is Now

Sometimes, like in the example just cited, life moves
forward at breakneck speed. Our battles come fast and

hard; sometimes it seems like we deal with one situation only to face another right on its heels. We would prefer long breaks and seasons of intermission, but most often that is not the case. Sometimes we know the giant is looming in the distance, but we would rather not confront the inevitable—at least not yet. There is no better time than now to confront what you will have to confront later. I'm not encouraging you to go looking for trouble. I'm speaking in reference to the things that you have simply procrastinated about. Just because something can wait, doesn't mean it *should* wait. Your growth as an individual may be on a permanent pause until you go and kill your giant.

Your doubt will not just magically disappear, your insecurities won't just fade away by themselves, and these giants are not in your life to defeat you, but to build you as you trust in Jesus. It's one thing to procrastinate about daily activities and time management issues, but it's an entirely different thing to prolong dealing with the major obstacles of your life. The time to kill your giant is now. The time to win is today, and the season of victory is here; stand up and kill your giant!

The time to kill your giant is now. The time to win is today, and the season of victory is here; stand up and kill your giant!

As discussed in Chapter 5, Goliath should have been killed by King Saul. After all, he was the king at the time, and the people were looking to him for leadership. Saul did not kill that giant. In fact, we don't have record of him killing any giants ever. These giants didn't disappear just because Saul chose to procrastinate over the inevitable, so God raised up a man who wouldn't procrastinate. David not only killed that giant, but was instrumental in killing all the remaining giants during his leadership.

Procrastination is a plague that not only kills productivity and spiritual growth, but it also undermines your purpose. What are you waiting for? Remember, the giants in your life have your name on them, and they have reared their ugly heads so you can grow and experience win after win. I was recently in a store and saw a sign hanging on the wall that read:

> If you do what you have to do,
> When you don't want to do it,
> Then one day
> You will be able to do,
> What you want to do, when you want to do it.

The giants of old don't just go away. They continue to reproduce if not snuffed out. The obstacles of your life—though you may not consider them as giants now— are quickly becoming bigger and harder to handle. What Saul refused to deal with in a timely manner, someone else had to confront. David understood that someone had to take on the giants. He thought: *Why not me, and why not now?* If we allow our fear to keep us from a head-on confrontation with the giants in our life, we will be missing out on a greater legacy, a more fulfilling existence, and opportunities yet to be seen.

It is time to face fear, self-doubt, and insecurity with a passion to win. When David was on the battlefield against Goliath, he knew this was his moment. There would be no turning back, no way to redeem a loss, and no way to move forward without a victory. We need to be like David. Stop making excuses and start killing your giant. Go get that job, start that business, get that degree, fix that broken relationship—start today by doing everything you can to demonstrate your trust in the Lord. Don't fall into the trap of trying to wait out your giant. Don't hope the giant gets so old that he no longer poses a threat. Challenge him, and challenge him immediately!

> It is time to face fear, self-doubt, and insecurity with a passion to win.

You have to believe that God put you on this earth during this time period for a reason. He is not powerless, He is not unavailable, and He is not against you. God is *for* your success, He believes in your future, and He knows that you have what it takes to succeed. God will be responsible for your victory, but you have to engage the fight. God didn't pick up David's sling for him. He didn't choose the rocks for him, and He didn't even trash-talk the giant for him. But when David did all he could do, God stepped in and directed that stone David hurled. With the accuracy of a digitally-planned missile

Chapter 10: Kill Your Giant!

launch, that stone hit the giant right in the forehead, striking him with a fatal blow. When you do your part to kill your giant, God will do what you can't and elevate your efforts to success!

I didn't write this book to give you head knowledge alone, but to encourage and equip you to take action. These words may be nothing more than just words, or these words can help you to slay your giant. The choice is yours, the power is in your hands, and the future awaits. There are giants out there waiting to be killed, waiting to show God's power, and waiting to be proof of your victory. Choose to transform your catastrophe into a catalyst. This catalyst is not about feeling good about yourself, it's about stepping into your future with the boldness and assurance that you are fulfilling your God-given potential.

> The giants don't exist to defeat you; they exist to be defeated by you.

The giants that are awaiting death have your name written on them. The giants don't exist to defeat you; they exist to be defeated *by you*. Don't let someone else steal your victory, and don't sell yourself short. The time is here, so don't postpone your celebration any longer. Move to your deeper purpose and the fulfillment of God's desire for you. You will succeed and you will not fail. If you've tried before, get up, dust yourself off, and try again. No more procrastination, no more excuses, no more dramatic sighs: Kill your giant!

10: Kill Your Giant
Action Points

Identify Your Giants: It's easy to make excuses about how you can't defeat your giant or how this giant is someone else's to confront. Honestly and truthfully, sit down and write a list of things you need to defeat. After you put it on paper, read the list aloud. Connect your faith verbally with the things you are believing for. There is something that happens as you do this. God will meet you in it.

Pray for Yourself: We don't usually need to be reminded to pray about our troubles, but we often fail to pray for ourselves. When you pray for yourself, ask the Lord to strengthen your faith, give you spiritual endurance, and help you remain faithful. Defeating giants takes a lot of personal grit, but it also requires a lot of faith.

Write a List of Past Victories: Take a few minutes and write down some things you've successfully accomplished or some obstacles you've defeated in the past. You may have to think hard, but write down even those battles that might seem insignificant to others. It could be something as simple as a diet you were on a few years ago when you lost ten pounds; that's a victory. Or job promotions, certifications, or educational milestones. These all count. Faith-building power comes with reciting your past victories. David did this when he faced Goliath. Remember how he recounted how he had killed bears and lions? Remembering these moments can help your faith grow and enable you to expect bigger gains in the future.

Make a Choice to Engage Your Giants Now: What can you do right now to move forward in attacking your giant? Is it a phone call, letter, investment, job application, interview, apology, or maybe something else altogether? Stop endlessly mulling over what to do, and do something, even if it's not perfect. Action creates action, and stagnation creates death. Whatever you can do immediately, do today; don't wait another day to move another step closer to victory.

Parting Words

This book was designed to be much more than a simple shot in the arm to encourage you to keep going. As a person who has experienced the ups and downs of life and many victories and defeats, encouraging and discouraging times, *I know the value of a process*. I would strongly encourage you to go back through this book from time to time and pay careful attention to any notes you may have made, as well as all of the Action Points.

God's plan is greater than you realize. Your ability is bigger than you know, and your future is brighter than you've ever imagined. Defeat the thing (or things) that are defeating you. You will be glad you did!

For Further Reading:

Foreword by Pat Schatzline

The Left-Handed

Warrior

Rise up and be the one nobody saw coming

"This book delivers
inspiration with a punch."
-Dr. Dave Martin

Jamie Jones

At a time in history when Israel desperately needed a deliverer, God chose an ordinary man—someone society had overlooked. He chose Ehud—a left-handed man who was daring enough to let God use his handicap to free a nation from Moabite oppression. The story of Ehud is one commonly passed over or forgotten, but it is much more than just the historical account of a biblical underdog victory. This is a story about God using regular people to do the unthinkable.

The Left-Handed Warrior is a story about people like you and me. Many times, the very thing that we've viewed as a handicap is actually the strategic plan of God to bring our success. Left-handed warriors were very uncommon, even viewed as weak and inferior in their day. For this specific task, God didn't choose just any warrior—He chose a left-handed warrior. Anyone else would have failed; anyone else would have been exposed. Anyone else wouldn't have been the left-handed warrior.

Our world is in need of left-handed warriors today—not actual stealth killers, but people who dream big dreams and accomplish impossible tasks. You may be the one they never saw coming! Inside each of us dwells incredible potential, incredible possibilities, and incredible exploits. I believe inside each of us there lies a left-handed warrior.

**For more information or to purchase,
visit www.jamiejonesministries.com.**

About the Author

Jamie Jones is the lead pastor at Trinity Church in Deltona, Florida. Under his leadership the church has seen tremendous growth and expansion. Pastor Jamie also oversees a network of pastors and churches in Western Honduras, and he and his wife, Michelle, travel to preach and teach about church leadership and revival. He is also the author of the recently published book *The Left-Handed Warrior*.

Contact us: www.jamiejonesministries.com.